Catching the Moments

Catching the Moments

STEVE ROTH

XULON PRESS

Xulon Press
2301 Lucien Way #415
Maitland, FL 32751
407. 339. 4217
www. xulonpress. com

Catching the Moments Introduction

"You saw me before I was born. Every day of my life was recorded in your book. Every moment was laid out before a single day had passed." Psalm 139:16 (NLT)

God has filled our lives with moments—special moments that He has recorded in His book. These moments were planned by God as He graciously inserted us into His incredible story. These moments are not all mountaintop experiences but were carefully crafted by our Creator before we were even born.

But here's the thing: sometimes we get so focused on ourselves that we don't see these moments for what they were intended to be. In fact, sometimes we miss them completely.

If our God has purposely inserted us into His eternal story and filled our days with these eternal moments, we should spend more time catching them. It is my prayer that the Holy Spirit will teach us how to capture these moments.

The daily devotions found within *Catching the Moments* comprise a collection of my personal thoughts and moments written over the last few years. I encourage you to intentionally catch more of the moments that our Heavenly Father has strategically placed in your life.

On Saturday of every week, a page is reserved for you to record those moments and Bible verses that were important to you during the previous week. Think of what you might collect after doing this for fifty-two weeks. You will not only have enough material to write your own devotional but may have a greater appreciation for what God has written in His book.

Catch the moments of your life. You are part of God's divine plan.

Jesus loves you.
Steve Roth

WEEK 1–SUNDAY

"This is the day the Lord has made; let us rejoice and be glad in it." Psalm 118:24 NIV84

Carpe diem! This exclamation is used to urge someone to make the most of the present time and give little thought the future. We may recognize the English version: seize the day!

This may sound like an odd New Year greeting, but let me ask you this: If you were to die tomorrow, how would your last full day on earth be written? Planning for the future is a wise thing to do, but it shouldn't be at the expense of forgetting *today*.

This is the day the Lord has made. We need to rejoice and be thankful for *this* day. It's a gift from God—take time to unwrap His gift! Before your head hits the pillow tonight, take time to identify the highlight of your day.

Get out of your funk! Thank your Heavenly Father for giving you this day. It is special. *Seize it!* And when you wake up tomorrow, seize that day also. Think of what this year would look like if we treated every day as a gift from God.

Let us rejoice! Take a moment to rejoice with someone else today.

WEEK 1–MONDAY

"May the words of my mouth and the meditation of my heart be pleasing in your sight, O Lord, my Rock and my Redeemer." Psalm 19:14 NIV84

I have been known to put my foot in my mouth from time to time. On occasion I have spoken some words that should have been seasoned with more grace, or better yet, I would have been far better off to just keep my mouth shut. For the longest time, I would respond by beating myself up and obsessing about how I could have chosen my words more wisely.

Through the years, God has been changing me. I still put my foot in my mouth from time to time, and when I'm wrong, I (usually) confess it quickly and get on with my life. That pleases my Redeemer. Even though my words may not be acceptable to others, I'm more concerned if they are acceptable to God. I'm changing, but I've also accepted who God has called me to be: a peculiar person who has been saved and redeemed by my Savior and Lord, Jesus Christ. I'm also learning to forgive others for the stupid things they may say.

Pause and think before you speak today.

WEEK 1–TUESDAY

"No one can snatch them out of my Father's hand." John 10:29b NIV84

I don't know about you, but there are times that I feel as though I'm losing my grip on God. That used to really bother me until I learned something essential to my faith: my faith does not rest upon how tight of a grip I have on God, but it's knowing that He has a tight grip on me.

Now, there are times I have to activate my faith and "get a grip," but when I hit one of those low moments, I am secure in the fact that there is nothing that can snatch me out of His hand. He has a grip on me and will never let go.

When my children were little, we would always hold hands when we crossed the street. Their safety was based upon how tight of a grip I had on them. That's what fathers do.

Your Father has got a grip on you, my friend. It's gonna be OK!

Start your day by picturing yourself in God's hand.

WEEK 1—WEDNESDAY

> *"See what great love the Father has lavished on us, that we should be called children of God! And that is what we are!"*
> *I John 3:1 NIV84*

God just doesn't give us *some* love; He has lavished His love on us. It is such an honor to be called a child of God, and that is who I am. Why? Because God's love was demonstrated in this incredible fact: While I was a sinful mess, He sent His Son, Jesus Christ, to die in my place. That incredible sacrifice made it possible for my sins to be forgiven and me to be accepted into the family of God.

God has lavished His love upon me so that I can lavish others with His love. Don't be content to merely be nice to someone today. Go out of your way to sacrifice and lavish someone else with God's love.

That's what God's children do. That is who we are.

Lavish: "bestow something in generous or extravagant quantities on."

WEEK 1—THURSDAY

> *"The Spirit himself testifies with our spirit that we are God's children." Romans 8:16 NIV84*

One Sunday, minutes before I was about to preach, I was overwhelmed with the following thoughts: *I don't know if the Bible is truly inspired by God. I don't know if I am forgiven. I don't know if I'm a child of God.*

For a brief moment I was shaken, but then the Holy Spirit, who dwelt within me, *rose up*. His voice was far more powerful, and I found myself boldly declaring that I was a child of God! I was forgiven and had a home waiting for me in heaven! I stood on the Word and, by faith, declared it to be true! It was one of those moments when *God just showed up.*

I am so thankful that the Holy Spirit lives and dwells within me. He gives me the assurance I am one of God's children. And my God doesn't like Satan messin' with one of His kids.

Be prepared to tell someone today who your Father is.

WEEK 1–FRIDAY

> *"I have been crucified with Christ and I no longer live, but Christ lives in me. The life I live in the body, I live by faith in the Son of God, who loved me and gave himself for me."*
> *Galatians 2:20 NIV84*

I would classify Galatians 2:20 as one of my *Life Verses*. It's not only one of my favorite scripture verses; it's one that guides my life and speaks to my heart over and over again. Over the years, I've gotten to know some of my friends' *Life Verses:*

- Leanor–Romans 15:13

- Petrina–Jeremiah 29:11

- Mona–Ephesians 3:20

- Lorraine–Isaiah 40:31

- Alison- Matthew 6:33

What about you? If you had to choose a *Life Verse*, what would it be? Let it be one that is easy to share and passes along an important message to others. A *Life Verse* is not more important than the rest of Scripture; it's just what the Holy Spirit has used to build your own personal faith.

There are 31,102 verses in the Bible. Name one that you cherish.

Catching the Moments

What moments stand out to you from this past week?

What verse of Scripture was important to you during the past week?

In seven words or fewer, describe this past week.

_____

_____

_____

_____

_____

_____

_____

_____

_____

_____

_____

_____

_____

WEEK 2-SUNDAY

"Because of the increase of wickedness, the love of most will grow cold." Matthew 24:12 NIV84

Jesus said that prior to His return, wickedness will increase. When that begins to happen, He said that the love of most will grow cold. Not the love of "some" but the love of "most." Friends, we need to be careful that our love for God and our love for others don't grow cold.

Sometimes the Church can do all the right things yet appear to be cold and uncaring in the process. Don't let that happen. Don't let wickedness desensitize your love for others.

Someone once asked Jesus what was the greatest commandment. His response: "Love the Lord your God with all your heart and with all your soul and with all your mind. This is the first and greatest commandment. And the second is like it: Love your neighbor as yourself." (Matt. 22:37–38)

Wickedness may be on the increase, but don't let your love grow cold. Don't ever let that happen!

Has your love grown cold toward anyone?

WEEK 2-MONDAY

"The glory of this latter temple shall be greater than the former," says the Lord of hosts. Haggai 2:9 NKJV

I believe the greatest days of the Church still lie ahead. Allow me to share some of my hopes about our future:

- The greatness of the future Church will not be seen in its numbers but in its faith.

- There will be a revival of the Great Commission in the individual lives of Christians.

- More people will be added to the Church through conversion, not through transferring of membership.

- More ministry will happen outside the walls of our local church facilities than happens inside our walls.

- A sense of awe will become common once again within the Church. People will be "blown away" by the displays of power Jesus shows within His Church.

- I believe the Church of the next generation will proudly identify themselves as Followers of Christ. The name of Jesus will unite the real Church and separate us from others.

- Love will transform lives on a daily basis.

Jesus, build Your Church!

WEEK 2–TUESDAY

"Blessed is the one who reads aloud the words of this prophecy, and blessed are those who hear it and take to heart what is written in it, because the time is near." Revelation 1:3 NIV84

Some people are afraid or at least hesitant to read the book of Revelation. But the above verse tells us that we will be blessed if we do. Even though I can't explain everything in the concluding book of the Bible, I am still blessed every time I read it. Please notice that it says "*blessed in the one who reads **aloud** the words of this prophecy*." Reading the Word of God aloud will bless the reader, the hearer, and the one who takes it to heart.

The time of Christ's return is near, so we need to take the words of this prophetic book to heart.

Don't be afraid of it. Don't be concerned if you don't understand all of it. Rejoice in what you read and understand. Jesus Christ is coming back.

When was the last time you read through the book of Revelation?

WEEK 2–WEDNESDAY

> *"Please listen, LORD God, and answer my prayers. Make my eyes sparkle again." Psalm 13:3 CEV*

There have been many times I have asked the Lord: How much longer? I didn't stop believing in Him or neglect the Body of Christ. I just lost the spiritual sparkle I used to have. I think you know what I mean. We've all been there.

One of the members of our congregation once told me she was doing fine, but I knew she was not. Something was wrong! When I gracefully confronted her, she asked me how I knew. I simply said, "You've lost your sparkle." She knew exactly what I meant.

What do we do to regain our sparkle? Look at what David said in verses 5 and 6 of Psalm 13. "But I trust in your unfailing love; my heart rejoices in your salvation. I will sing the Lord's praise, for he has been good to me." Follow David's example, and you will get your sparkle back.

Trust! Rejoice! Sing! And sparkle!

Have your eyes lost their spiritual sparkle?

WEEK 2–THURSDAY

> *"When the people of the land come before the Lord at the appointed festivals, whoever enters by the north gate to worship is to go out by the south gate; and whoever enters by*

the south gate is to go out the north gate. No one is to return through the gate by which they entered." Ezekiel 46:9 NIV 84

I love this passage of scripture because it tells us what can happen when we return from worshipping the Lord. It says the people should be leaving by a different gate. In short, we should not return from worship the way we came.

Something happens when we worship the Lord, whether it is with a group or by ourselves. There have been those times I entered the church facilities with a downcast spirit but left on a spiritual high. What made the difference? It was usually worship! Just singing a song does not touch the heart of God, but true worship does.

We should not return from worship the way we came.

Worship is not something we get on Sunday morning; it's something we bring.

WEEK 2—FRIDAY

"So pray to the Lord of the harvest to force out and thrust laborers into His harvest." Matthew 9:38 AMP.

Jesus is telling His disciples the spiritual harvest is plentiful and needs workers *now*! So Jesus instructed them to start praying for laborers to be forced out and thrust into action.

Many versions accurately say that we should ask the Lord of the harvest to send out workers. The Amplified Version just gives a stronger meaning to the word "send." All too often, we use the excuse that we are not ready to labor in God's kingdom. That's why Jesus told His followers that, starting with themselves, they needed to boldly pray: Lord, force me out into service. Thrust me into action!

The best form of discipleship is "hands-on." While training and teaching are essential, Jesus seems to be saying that the Church needs more workers, not trainees. We've already been gifted with the Holy Spirit, so step into the harvest field and let God use you.

Have you ever been thrust into a ministering opportunity?

Catching the Moments

What moments stand out to you from this past week?

What verse of Scripture was important to you during the past week?

In seven words or fewer, describe this past week.

_____

_____

_____

_____

_____

_____

_____

_____

_____

_____

WEEK 3–SUNDAY

> *"Lord, when you favored me, you made my royal mountain stand firm." Psalm 30:7 NIV84*

Sometimes the Bible refers to mountains as a place of stability (see Psalm 30:7). There are other times a mountain is referred to as an obstacle (see Zechariah 4:7). There are mountains that we are called to climb (see Matthew 17:1) and other mountains we are told to move by speaking to them in faith (Matt. 17:20).

Identify your mountain! Is the mountain you are facing a place of stability, or is it an obstacle? Does God want you to climb it or speak to it? We need more spiritual discernment. Is my mountain something I must accept or reject?

The Lord has favored you by placing mountains in your path. What is the purpose for which the Lord has put those mountains in your life? Don't overcomplicate the discernment process. Just ask the Lord, and then be obedient.

If you had to name your mountain, what would it be?

WEEK 3–MONDAY

> *"I will pour out my Spirit on your offspring, and my blessing on your descendants." Isaiah 44:3 NIV84*

God is not done with your family, so don't give up on them. He wants to pour out His Spirit on your children and bring salvation to those family members who don't know Jesus. Persevere in prayer for them. Love them with the love God has showered on you. One day, one of your children will say "I belong to the Lord" and another will get a tattoo on his hand, "The Lord's." (see Isaiah 44:5). Think of the joy that is waiting for you when your loved ones come to believe in Jesus.

If you do not have children, God has called us to be spiritual parents to others within the Body of Christ. Let the confession of Isaiah 44:3 be on your mouth. Ask the Lord to pour out His Spirit on your children and allow His blessing to fall upon those family members who are not saved.

Oh, and when you ask the Lord to pour out His Spirit, ask Him to start with you.

Ask the Lord to pour out His Spirit through you and let it touch your offspring.

WEEK 3—TUESDAY

> *"Be faithful until death, and I will give you the crown of life."*
> *Revelation 2:10 NKJV*

This was the verse given to me on my Confirmation Day by my pastor (and father) in 1963. I have never forgotten this wonderful verse over all these years. I can't help but think that it was carefully chosen by Dad, and I am so thankful for the joy it gives me. Not only the joy that awaits me in heaven but the fact that Steven means "crown."

Stay faithful, my friends, not just for a season. Be faithful until you die, because there is a reward waiting for us that we can't even imagine. When you are plagued with doubts, stay faithful. When finances are at an all-time low, stay faithful. When sickness has robbed you of your independence, stay faithful. When family and friends hurt you, stay faithful.

Never underestimate the importance of remaining faithful to our God. He hasn't called us to be successful; He has called us to be faithful. When we are, He always rewards us.

In what area are you weak in faithfulness?

> *"My house will be called a house of prayer for all nations."*
> *Isaiah 56:7b NIV84*

God wants His house to be called a house of prayer. What do people call the house where your church meets? Does prayer have a priority in its function? Do outsiders say, "The people who attend here are committed to prayer"? God also wants His house to be a place where people from all nations gather. That means He wants His house to be diverse. Clearly, there are those who say they want more diversity within the Church, but fewer are willing to cross racial barriers for it to happen. Many say, "The Church is very diverse—they have their churches and we have ours." I don't think that is what the Lord had in mind.

Talk with others about how the Church can be more committed to prayer and more committed to diversity. Your neighborhood may not be ethnically diverse, but you can still be a positive voice in a racially divided Church. As we remember the life of Martin Luther King Jr., you can honor his memory by being an agent of change.

"Our lives begin to end the day we become silent about things that matter."—MLK Jr.

> *"And it came to pass." Joshua 4:1 NKJV*

These five words are found many times throughout the Bible. To me, they are very encouraging words that help me to persevere and keep on going. God has a plan and purpose for everyone of us, and all He asks is that we trust Him.

"And it came to pass" signifies a moment that God was about to do something. In the preceding verse the people of God had just crossed the Jordan into the Promised Land, and now they were instructed to build a memorial to remember this important event in their lives. Very simply, the memorial stones were to say, "We trusted God . . . and it came to pass."

Are you going through a difficult period in your life? You need to trust in the Lord, and it will come to pass. God keeps all His promises, and they always come to pass. If someone should ask you why you have so much hope, just tell them, "And it came to pass."

The phrase "and it came to pass" is used 396 times in the King James Version.

WEEK 3—FRIDAY

> *"On the Lord's Day I was in the Spirit, and I heard behind me a loud voice." Revelation 1:10 NIV84*

Many Christian historians interpret "the Lord's Day" to be the first day of the week, the day our Lord Jesus rose from the dead. I like to think the Lord's Day can best be compared to our Sunday—the day when we gather to worship our Lord.

The Apostle John had been abandoned to the isle of Patmos because of the word of God and his testimony of Jesus. Even in this remote place of punishment, John observed the Lord's Day. Take it a step further; he was in the Spirit of the Lord's Day.

Church, please pay attention that John observed the Lord's Day until the day he died. He didn't stay home and sleep in on Sunday or complain that the music was too contemporary. He was in the Spirit.

Next Sunday, ask the Lord to help you get in the Spirit as you travel to your local congregation. You just may hear from God.

What do you think it means to be "in the Spirit"?

Catching the Moments

What moments stand out to you from this past week?

What verse of Scripture was important to you during the past week?

In seven words or fewer, describe this past week.

_____

_____

_____

_____

_____

_____

_____

_____

_____

_____

_____

_____

_____

> *"No, dear brothers and sisters, I have not achieved it, but I focus on this one thing: Forgetting the past and looking forward to what lies ahead." Philippians 3:13 NLT*

I have a good friend, Mona, who has the reputation of getting others to *focus*. From time to time, I need that reminder.

Focus refers to paying particular attention to a subject, object, or person. The Apostle Paul stated the importance of focusing on moving forward in his relationship with the Lord and not getting stuck in the past. Satan is good at distracting us from what is important. He knows that if we are paying attention to many things, we can lose our effectiveness. And he knows if I become locked into my failures and successes of the past, my ability to focus will be hindered.

Focus on this one thing: what lies ahead. God has many blessings and divine appointments waiting for each of us. Even though you are able to multitask, learn how to focus.

Ask God to give you strength to let go of the past and move forward into new places of grace.

> *Jesus answered, "If I want him to remain alive until I return, what is that to you? You must follow me." John 21:22 NIV84*

The Risen Jesus had just asked Peter to follow Him to where he would not want to go on his own. Peter noticed that Jesus had not extended the same challenging call to John, who was with them, so he said, "What about him?"

I love Jesus's response (something He has said to me on more than one occasion): "What is that to you? You must follow me." Put that same scenario in the present-day Church. Sometimes we may feel that the Lord is calling us to do something that is not appealing while neglecting to call someone else. *What about him, Lord? Why are you calling me and not someone else?*

"What is that to you? You must follow Me." Does that sound kind of hard? Shouldn't Jesus have been more considerate of my feelings? Our willingness to follow Jesus should never be based upon who goes with us. Don't compare your calling with someone else's.

There is no safer place to be than in the center of God's will.

WEEK 4—TUESDAY

> *"Epaphras, who is one of you and a servant of Christ Jesus, sends greetings. He is always wrestling in prayer for you, that you may stand firm in all the will of God, mature and fully assured." Colossians 4:12NIV84*

Epaphras is someone I would like to call a prayer warrior—someone who not only prayed for others but wrestled in prayer for them. Prayer warriors are not your run-of-the-mill Christians; they would most likely be viewed as fanatics. Those who wrestle in prayer for others are willing to get emotionally involved in their prayers and willing to empathize with those they are praying for. They could be very quiet and gentle people, but once they enter into prayer, they are transformed into wrestlers.

I have the utmost respect for believers who are like Epaphras. It is their prayers that help me to stand firm in the will of God when I'm going through a hard time. Their prayers are what help me mature and be assured of God's presence in my life. Take time to thank an Epaphras in your life.

Have you ever wrestled in prayer for someone else?

WEEK 4—WEDNESDAY

"For it is by grace you have been saved, through faith—and this not from yourselves, it is the gift of God." Ephesians 2:8 NIV84

What is it that sets Christianity apart from all the other religions in the world? *Grace.* Jesus Christ paid the price for your sin and gave us eternal life *by grace.* All He asks is that we believe in Him. Our salvation is an incredible gift given to us by God, yet there are so many who refuse to accept it.

We are not saved by merely going to church; we are not saved by becoming a member of the *right* denomination; we are not saved by merely being baptized or confirmed; we are not saved by performing many good deeds. We are saved *only* by grace through faith in Jesus Christ. The law makes us aware that we are sinful and unsaved, but Grace brings us forgiveness and the salvation we so desperately need.

Those who have been touched by the grace of God find it much easier to give it away.

We need grace every day. We never become grace graduates.

WEEK 4 -THURSDAY

"I will give you a new heart and put a new spirit in you; I will remove from you your heart of stone and give you a heart of flesh." Ezekiel 36:26 NIV84

When I was in my mid-fifties I had a splenectomy. The problem wasn't my spleen; it was what was growing inside of it. I had a large abscess that had grown inside my spleen, and if it broke, it could have serious consequences for me. So the surgeon told me that the only way to safely remove the abscess was to remove the spleen. The surgery was successful, and I have had no side effects.

When each of us is born, we are born with a deadly growth inside of us. It's not always visible; in fact, some of us can hide it quite well. The only answer is for the sinful growth to be removed. The only one who can successfully remove that growth is Jesus. When He performs His spiritual surgery, we are given a new life and new hope.

Lord, thank You for removing my heart of stone.

WEEK 4–FRIDAY

> *"Until I come, devote yourself to the public reading of Scripture, to preaching and to teaching." I Timothy 4:13 NIV84*

One of the many traditions that I cherish in the Lutheran Church is the Lectionary Series. A lectionary is a collection of readings from Scripture that are arranged according to the Church's calendar and are intended to be publicly read at the regular, weekly gathering of God's people. It usually contains readings from the Old Testament, an Epistle, and a Gospel reading. When people are devoted to the reading of the Word and do so with reverence and respect, it has a tremendous effect on the hearers.

Many of my sermons have come from the assigned reading for the day, but even when I do not use them as a text for the sermon, faith can come to those who just listen to the Word of God being read (Rom. 10:17)

I pray that your congregation is devoted to the public reading of Scripture each week. And if you have the opportunity to be one of the readers, do it with reverence and respect.

Have you ever had the honor to publicly read the Word of God in Church?

Catching the Moments

What moments stand out to you from this past week?

What verse of Scripture was important to you during the past week?

In seven words or fewer, describe this past week.

_____

_____

_____

_____

_____

_____

_____

_____

_____

_____

_____

_____

_____

_____

> *"Jesus went throughout Galilee, teaching in their synagogues, proclaiming the good news of the kingdom, and healing every disease and sickness among the people." Matthew 4:23 NIRV*

Jesus still heals disease and sickness among the people today, but now He does it through His Church. We are not the source of healing, just the agents through which it flows. He has given us the authority and the command to go in His name and lay hands on the sick.

Don't be afraid to lay your hands on the sick and pray for the Lord's healing. We don't need more training; we need more boldness to just step out and "do it." There is nothing quite like the experience of seeing the Lord bring healing to someone you have laid your hands on. There is a rush of spiritual confidence that may enter your life when you realize that God has just answered a prayer.

There is a world of sick people who are in need of healing. As the Lord presents the opportunity, expect Him to heal someone that you pray for.

Pay attention today. Opportunities to pray are waiting.

WEEK 5–MONDAY

> *"'But what about you?' he asked. 'Who do you say I am?' Peter answered, 'You are the Messiah.'" Mark 8:29 NIRV*

Jesus had just asked His disciples to share with Him "Who do people say I am?" They answered Him by sharing the secondhand information they had heard. Some thought Jesus was John the Baptist, others thought He was Elijah, and still others thought He was one of the prophets. But then Jesus cut to the chase: "What about you? Who do you say I am?"

In other words, *don't tell me what others are saying; answer for yourself. Tell me, personally, who I am in your life.* Peter nailed it: "You are the Messiah."

What about you, my friend? Who do you say Jesus is in your life? You've got to answer for yourself—from your own heart. It's not what your pastor says or your parents say. *Who do you say Jesus is?*

When you finally open your mouth and make that personal confession, Jesus does something special in your heart.

When was the last time you told Jesus who He is in your life?

WEEK 5—TUESDAY

> *"After the Lord had said these things to Job, he said to Eliphaz the Temanite, 'I am angry with you and your two friends, because you have not spoken the truth about me, as my servant Job has.'" Job 42:7 NIRV*

Eliphaz and his two friends were good at preaching at Job but were of little help in standing with him. They assumed that Job had been rebellious toward God because they believed if we are obedient, He will bless us, protect us, and keep us from suffering. They were full of answers to Job's problems, but they were of no help. Job didn't need cut-and-dried theological answers to his suffering; he needed some compassionate friends.

If you have friends who are going through some hard times, don't misrepresent God. Your friends do not need the right theological answers; they need someone who will show them the love of a merciful God. Even though Job had his moments of venting, he never lost his faith in God.

Love your suffering friends and speak the truth about God.

Thank a friend who has stood with you in hard times.

WEEK 5—WEDNESDAY

"When Elijah heard it, he pulled his cloak over his face and went out and stood at the mouth of the cave." I Kings 19:13 NIV84

Elijah, the great prophet of the Lord, had run away in fear and found himself hiding in a cave. God had told him to come out of his cave into His presence, but it didn't happen right away. First, the Lord sent a great and powerful wind that tore the mountain apart, but the Lord was not in the wind . . . and Elijah stayed in the cave. After that an earthquake, but the Lord was not in it . . . and Elijah stayed in the cave. Next was a fire, but the Lord was not in it . . . and Elijah stayed in the cave. Finally, God spoke in a gentle whisper, which made Elijah cover his face and come out of the cave.

Fear has driven me to hide out in a few caves of my own. It was the gentle whisper of the Holy Spirit and His still, small voice that brought me out. The gentle whisper of God is a powerful force.

Is God calling you out of a cave?

WEEK 5—THURSDAY

"All praise to the God and Father of our Master, Jesus the Messiah! Father of all mercy! God of all healing counsel! He comes alongside us when we go through hard times, and before you know it, he brings us alongside someone else who is going through hard times so that we can be there for that person just as God was there for us." 2 Corinthians 1:3–4 MSG

According to *The Message*, God's comfort means to come alongside us. When I go through hard times, it is extremely comforting to know that my God has come alongside me. The hard times are still there, but I know that I will get through them because God is really with me. Then, after I get through those hard times, He will bring me alongside someone else who is going through some hard times.

Sometimes you don't even have to speak. Your mere presence makes a difference. I am thankful for a Savior who still comes alongside us. The Holy Spirit can work through your mere presence.

God comforts us so that we can become comforters.

WEEK 5-FRIDAY

> *"May they be brought to complete unity to let the world know that you sent me and have loved them even as you have loved me." John 17:23 NIV84*

God, the Father, loves us as much as He loves Jesus. *Wow!* I used to have a hard time accepting that fact. After all, who am I compared to Jesus? Our Heavenly Father was willing to sacrifice His only begotten Son (whom He loved) for us, whom He loves just as much. Isn't that incredible?

We like to measure the strength of our love in degrees. But God's love isn't like that. Love is not something God *does*; it is something He *is*. His love is always seeking nothing but the highest good for all those who were created in His image. He demonstrated that love by sending His own Son to the cross—for us!

When we are brought to complete unity as His redeemed children, the world will not only begin to see the love of God; they will begin to know the love of God.

God's love for me is not based on my performance.

Catching the Moments

What moments stand out to you from this past week?

What verse of Scripture was important to you during the past week?

In seven words or fewer, describe this past week.

_____

_____

_____

_____

_____

_____

_____

_____

_____

_____

_____

_____

WEEK 6—SUNDAY

"He put a new song in my mouth, a hymn of praise to our God."
Psalm 40:3 NIV84

A new song is not necessarily one we have never heard before. It actually could be a song we have heard many times before. An "old" song can become a "new" song when we allow the Holy Spirit to bring a spiritual freshness to our worship. It can be an old, familiar hymn from the past; a new, contemporary chorus; a choir anthem; or a spontaneous song of praise that flows from our heart. It could be sung in the fellowship of other believers or alone by yourself.

It's amazing how two people can be singing the same song in a worship service, but to one it is old and dead and to the other it is new and fresh. Don't criticize the old songs that others may be singing. Enjoy the privilege of worshipping your God with a new song.

A new song becomes a hymn of praise when we put words to the song that was planted in our hearts by God Himself.

God will put a new song in my mouth, but it's up to me to open my mouth.

WEEK 6—MONDAY

"Abraham called that place The Lord Will Provide. And to this day it is said, 'On the mountain of the Lord it will be provided.'" Genesis 22:14 NIV84

God tested Abraham's faith by asking him to sacrifice his only son. Abraham believed, and it was credited to him as righteousness. God provided.

God sacrificed His only Son on a mountain called Calvary, and to those who believe, it is credited to them as righteousness. God provided.

Don't be afraid of the mountain you may be facing. Some mountains are meant to be moved and others are meant to be climbed. God is testing your faith, but He will provide. Just as He provided a lamb for Abraham, He provided a Lamb for us. God's provision is found within the lamb that takes away the sin of the world. He has promised to provide for all our needs through His Son, Jesus Christ our Lord.

Look at the problem you are currently facing and say these words: *the Lord will provide.*

Jehovah Jireh *means "The Lord will provide."*

WEEK 6—TUESDAY

> *"Those who hope in the Lord will renew their strength. They will soar on wings like eagles." Isaiah 40:31 NIRV*

A farmer captured an eagle and kept it tethered in his barnyard with the chickens. Months later, one of the farmer's friends rebuked him for imprisoning this creature and urged him to set the eagle free. The farmer was convicted of his cruelty and decided to untie the rope holding the eagle captive. However, the eagle stayed put in the barnyard scratching at the ground with the chickens. You see, he had lived so long among the chickens that he had forgotten how to be an eagle.

The farmer decided to take this eagle up on the side of the mountain and throw him off. He concluded that the eagle needed to be encouraged to do what it was created to do—*soar*. The eagle soon found himself flapping his wings, trying to avoid hitting the ground. And then, instinctively, he locked his wings in place and found himself soaring. **Before you can soar, sometimes you have to be thrown.**

Have you ever experienced what it is like to spiritually soar?

> *"When Jacob awoke from his sleep, he thought, 'Surely the Lord is in this place, and I was not aware of it.'"* **Genesis 28:16 NIV84**

Jacob was alone and spent the night in a lonely and dark place, but after waking from an incredible dream, he realized the presence of the Lord was all around him . . . but he hadn't known it. His encounter with God was so awesome that he named the place *Bethel* ("house of God").

How many times have you been in a lonely and dark place and longed for the presence of the Lord? He is there! He is always there! We are just not aware of it.

When you get into one of those places, let the Lord speak to you through His Word. Read what He told Jacob in preceding verses. I especially like what He said in verse 15: "I will not leave you until I have done what I have promised you."

The presence of the Lord is with you, even if you are not aware of it. And He will never leave you until He has done all that He has promised.

How can you increase your awareness of God's presence?

> *"These are the numbers of the men armed for battle who came to David at Hebron to turn Saul's kingdom over to him, as the Lord as said: from Issachar, men who understood the times and knew what Israel should do."* **I Chronicles 12:23, 32 NIRV**

The men of Issachar have always fascinated me—they understood the times and knew what Israel should do. We need more "Men of Issachar" in the Church. There are those whom God has blessed with wisdom to understand our current culture, to interpret current events, and to discern the signs of the times. God doesn't always expect us to become like the culture we live in. He does expect us to understand it.

As the Church continues to ask the Lord "What should we do?" maybe one of His responses would be, "Why don't you make an effort to understand the people who live in your community?" If you are stuck in the past, it might not be a bad idea to surround yourself with some people of Issachar.

The seven last words of a dying church: We Never Did It That Way Before.

WEEK 6-FRIDAY

> *"Therefore, there is now no condemnation for those who are in Christ Jesus." Romans 8:1 NIV84*

It is incredibly burdensome to live under condemnation. Satan is good at condemning us even after we come to faith in Jesus Christ as our Lord and Savior. Scripture even calls him "the accuser of the brethren." When Jesus died upon that cross, He took all of my sins upon Himself and took my punishment so that I would no longer have to live under condemnation.

If we have confessed our sins to our Lord, He has forgiven us. Maybe it's time you forgive yourself. Keep yourself in Christ Jesus. Don't let the enemy condemn you when your God has forgiven you.

The freedom we get to enjoy was bought and paid for by the blood of Jesus. That's the meaning of grace! Although the grace of our God is free, it is not cheap. Don't ever take your spiritual freedom for granted. Thank the Lord today that you don't have to live under condemnation anymore.

Whenever you see a "therefore" in Scripture, you should ask yourself, "What is it there for?"

Catching the Moments

What moments stand out to you from this past week?

What verse of Scripture was important to you during the past week?

In seven words or fewer, describe this past week.

_____

_____

_____

_____

_____

_____

_____

_____

_____

_____

_____

> *"We preach Christ crucified: a stumbling block to the Jews and foolishness to Gentiles." I Corinthians 1:23NIV84*

Christ crucified—that needs to be the central message of the Church. Without that central message, there would be no Church. Whenever I visit a new church, that is always the message I listen for. It doesn't have to be the topic of the sermon, but it must be the foundation of what a congregation is built upon. I once left a worship service where most people were extremely hyped up over the experience of the message and the music. I was saddened, because there was no mention of the cross or Jesus.

A church once had this sign out front: **We Preach Christ Crucified**. They began to neglect the physical appearance of their facilities, and hedges grew over the sign until you could only read, **We Preach Christ**. The hedges continued to take over the sign until you could only read **We Preach**. Finally, you guessed it, the sign only read **We**.

That is what can happen to a church when they neglect its spiritual purpose.

Trust in the One who died for you.

> *"Though outwardly we are wasting away, yet inwardly we are being renewed day by day." 2 Corinthians 4:16 NIV84*

Alison's brother, Robert, spent the last several months of his life living in our home. In his earlier drug addiction years, he had been infected with AIDS through some unclean needles. Even though he had been delivered from that addiction, the effects of those years caught up with him. In 1990 AIDS was viewed by many as a modern-day leprosy. Needless to say, we had fewer visitors to our house. While precautions were taken and round-the-clock nursing accompanied the last weeks of his life, it was hard watching the deterioration of Robert's physical body. Outwardly he was wasting away, but inwardly he was being renewed.

In his healthy years, Robert sometimes gave Alison a hard time about Christianity, but his life in Christ came alive during his last days on earth. That was a difficult season for our whole family, but if we had to do it all over, we'd do it again.

Don't lose sight of the inner life of someone who is dying.

I believe there is a renewal that takes place in a believer's heart prior to death.

WEEK 7—TUESDAY

> *"But God demonstrates his own love for us in this: While we were still sinners, Christ died for us." Romans 5:8 NIRV*

God doesn't just say that He loves us; He demonstrates His love. He showed us how much He loves us by sacrificing His own Son to suffer and die in our place.

On Valentine's Day people try to express their love for others through Valentine's Day cards, boxes of chocolate, and bouquets of flowers. While God's love can be demonstrated in simple ways (and should be), our love for one another needs to go beyond a box of Whitman's Chocolates. In fact, do something today that demonstrates the power of God's love; do something that costs you something (and I'm not talking money). Demonstrate the love of God to someone who doesn't like you. Demonstrate the love of God to someone who doesn't go to Church. God's love is demonstrated to people who don't deserve it.

It took me a long time to understand this: while I was still a sinner, Christ died for me.

Love is characterized by action more than affection.

WEEK 7—WEDNESDAY

> *"One of you routs a thousand, because the Lord your God fights for you, just as he promised." Joshua 23:10 NIRV*

Never underestimate the power of one person—under the power of One God. Throughout history God specialized in using one person to make a difference in this world.

- One shepherd boy named David—he was delivering food to some soldiers and ended up killing a giant.

- One monk named Martin—he was seeking forgiveness for his own sins and ended up starting a reformation.

- One passenger named Rosa—she was just sitting on a bus and ended up a civil rights hero.

God has put you on this earth for a purpose and is able to use you—insignificant and unknown—to accomplish His eternal purpose. One person can rout a thousand, influence a thousand, or teach a thousand. When your time comes, will you be ready? You might not change the course of history for the world, but you can change it for one other person. Never underestimate the power of one. You and God make a majority.

Your life can make a difference!

WEEK 7—THURSDAY

> *"For he will command his angels concerning you to guard you in all your ways." Psalm 91:11 NIV84*

I thank God for my guardian angels. I really do! We have each been assigned some ministering spirits to guard us in *all* our ways. They just don't guard us when we do what is right, but they especially guard when we do something stupid. I can just imagine God commanding my guardian angel, "Pay extra attention to Steve today, because he is going to do something stupid."

When I was twelve years old, Eddie and I spent a lot of time together doing what we did best: getting into trouble. On one occasion, we went in his backyard, took our bow and arrows, shot them straight in the air, and ran for cover in his house. Some of them landed where we were standing and others landed on the roof of his house. When his mother saw what we were doing, she asked us that question only angry mothers can ask:"What are you, stupid?"

Yes, we were, and God's angels kept those arrows from landing in our heads. Thank God for your angels today.

Jesus was not an angel, nor do we become angels.

WEEK 7–FRIDAY

> *"Repent, then, and turn to God, so that your sins may be wiped out, that times of refreshing may come from the Lord."*
> *Acts 3:19 NIV84*

Ash Wednesday is the first day of the season of Lent. It is also the day of Mardi Gras. These two dates coincide because I'm told that one of the reasons for Mardi Gras is that we should party as much as we can because Lent is coming. Hmmm. I haven't found that verse in the Bible yet.

Repentance is a good thing. Did you know that? John the Baptist preached repentance. So did Jesus and the early Church. They emphasized repentance because when we truly repent of our sins, it can lead to times of refreshing. There is nothing more refreshing than having my sins completely wiped out. Religion is complicated, but faith is simple: Jesus died for my sins and through repentance I am reconciled to God.

Turn to God. God's grace is amazing and free; it's not cheap. Ash Wednesday can lead to a time of partying but only when we turn our back on sin.

Repentance can be like a cool wind on a hot day.

WEEK 7—SATURDAY

Catching the Moments

What moments stand out to you from this past week?

What verse of Scripture was important to you during the past week?

In seven words or fewer, describe this past week.

_____

_____

_____

_____

_____

_____

_____

_____

"Continue to remember those in prison as if you were together with them in prison." Hebrews 13:3 NIV84

Our congregation used to have a prison ministry where we would go to Riker's Island once a month. At this correctional facility—behind LaGuardia Airport—there were more than twenty thousand inmates. It was quite an experience traveling over that bridge and then passing multiple checkpoints until finally arriving at one of the chapels. After having a short opening time of song and prayer, at the urging of the chaplain, we split into smaller groups. Our volunteers would then coordinate a discussion around a particular topic and close in prayer. At first it was a bit intimidating, but once we got to know the men, it was a blessing to see how God met these transparent men.

Once the chaplain put things in perspective by asking me the following question:"Do you know the only difference between many of these men and you?" His answer:"They got caught and you didn't."

If you know someone in prison, why not send them a card? It's only because of God's grace that some of us are not behind bars.

We all have our prisons where we need others to remember us.

"Look! I see four men walking around in the fire, unbound and unharmed, and the fourth looks like a son of the gods." Daniel 3:25 NIV84

Are you looking for a promotion? Look at Shadrach, Meshach, and Abednego. They were thrown into the fire because they were not willing to compromise their love for God. But when Nebuchadnezzar looked into the furnace, he not only saw the three of them—free and unharmed—he also saw Jesus walking around with them. They found their freedom *in* the fire.

They were already free and unharmed when they came out of the fire, but then God blessed them even further. "Then the king promoted Shadrach, Meshach, and Abednego in the province of Babylon." (3:30)

Maybe you have been thrown into the fire on your job. Don't despair. When you allow Jesus to meet you, true freedom can keep you free and unharmed. Others are watching how you will react.

Jesus not only wants to bring you out of the fire, He wants to bring you out with a testimony. You may even get a promotion in the process.

Stop looking for freedom outside of your problems.

WEEK 8–TUESDAY

> *"You call out to God for help and he helps—he's a good Father that way. But don't forget, he's also a responsible Father, and won't let you get by with sloppy living." I Peter 1:17 MSG*

I was blessed to have a good and responsible earthly father. I loved him for how he would put his hand on my shoulder when I was in need of some affirmation. I respected him for how that same hand would occasionally land on my behind when I was in need of discipline. I loved my dad.

I love my Heavenly Father even more. He is always good to me and always helps me in my time of need. However, I have learned to respect His authority also, because He does not want my spiritual walk to become sloppy. Occasionally it does, but my Responsible Father also shows His goodness through discipline.

"Sloppy Agape" is not a good witness to a hurting and fearful world. Ask the Lord where you may have gotten sloppy, and then call out to Him for His help. He's a good Father.

Our Heavenly Father is responsible. Thank Him for that quality today.

WEEK 8—WEDNESDAY

> *"Don't be afraid of them. Remember the Lord, who is great and awesome, and fight for your families, your sons and your daughters, your wives and your homes." Nehemiah 4:14 NIRV*

Our families are being taken captive. They may be living under the same roof, but the enemy is subtly robbing the family unit of the power they used to have. We were never perfect, but there was a time when the mother and father were respected; families used to eat together at the table and there were consequences for bad behavior. It's not going to change overnight, so what do we do?

First, don't let fear shape your family. Second, remember the Lord, for He is great and awesome. Third, fight for your families—not physically but spiritually... on your knees. Parents, make the decision to be godly examples who are willing to pray together, eat together, laugh together, love together, and worship together. Drastic problems require drastic solutions, and a family that is founded upon the love of God is able to overcome. Fight for your marriage and your family.

If your family is broken or divided, fight for them ... not with them!

WEEK 8—THURSDAY

> *"I waited patiently for the Lord; he turned to me and heard my cry." Psalm 40:1 NIV84*

I'm still learning how to wait patiently for the Lord to act in some areas of my life. Waiting has more to do with our attitude than our activity. I'm good at activity but not always at attitude. Just stopping my busy activity does not mean I've mastered the art of waiting for the Lord. The dictionary gives this definition of the word *wait*: "to remain inactive in readiness or expectation." Do we have an attitude of readiness or expectation while we are waiting on the Lord?

I was once told that the Hebrew term for "waited" in the preceding verse actually translates, "I waited-waited." The teacher explained it in this way: "Doubling of a term in Hebrew conveys an intensified meaning of the word."

Don't lose sight of the last half of this verse: He turns to us and hears us when we learn how to wait-wait. Be ready-ready and expect-expect our Lord to hear your cry for help.

Try to imagine God turning His face toward you and hearing your cry for help.

WEEK 8–FRIDAY

> *"Be wise in the way you act towards outsiders: make the most of every opportunity." Colossians 4:5 NIV84*

It is extremely important that we use wisdom in how we act toward everyone we meet. Those who are not believers in Jesus Christ will never want to hear our message if our first impression is unappealing. You've probably heard the expression "We never have a second chance to leave a first impression."

Whenever I am standing in line at Walmart, the bank, or the grocery store, God may be giving me an opportunity to make a good first impression. Sometimes we make the mistake of giving off an angry, unhappy, or grumpy first impression. Other times, our first impression may open a door for conversation.

Ask the Lord to give you wisdom today in how you act toward outsiders. Ask Him to make the most of every opportunity you may have to make a first impression. Before they are willing to hear the message, they might need to accept the messenger. A good start is to be kind and considerate, and to put a smile on our face.

Ask the Holy Spirit to remind you how to act toward other people today.

Catching the Moments

What moments stand out to you from this past week?

What verse of Scripture was important to you during the past week?

In seven words or fewer, describe this past week.

_____

_____

_____

_____

_____

_____

_____

_____

_____

> *"But the Lord is in his holy temple; let all the earth be silent before him." Habakkuk 2:20 NIV84*

In our worship and praise of God, there are times we should shout, dance, clap our hands, and be clamorously foolish. Then there are other times we need to be silent and absorb His holy presence. I'm learning the art of keeping my mouth shut and allowing our Mighty God to reveal Himself to me. This is especially true in the morning, when I spend time alone reading, praying, and journaling. In the midst of my quiet time, I become more aware that the Lord is present in His holy temple.

"Don't you know that you yourselves are God's temple and that God's Spirit lives in you?" (I Cor. 3:16). Jesus Christ has sent His Holy Spirit to live within me. There are times that makes me want to shout; other times it makes me want to be silent; and still others times (God forgive me), I forget.

God is in His holy temple. Absorb His presence today.

Ask the Lord to teach you how to be silent.

> *"Now, Lord, consider their threats and enable your servants to speak your word with great boldness. Stretch out your hand to heal and perform miraculous signs and wonders through the name of your holy servant Jesus." Acts 4:29–30 NIV84*

Even though they had been forbidden to teach any longer in Jesus's name, the disciples asked the Lord for an even greater boldness to teach, preach, and be vessels of His miraculous signs and wonders. They asked the Lord for a "holy audacity."

Audacity is the willingness to take bold risks. It wasn't enough for them to stay put and worship together. They wanted to go out in the name of Jesus and show the world that He is still alive. If you study the prayers of the early Church, they often were centered on becoming more powerful and effective witnesses for Jesus. Today our prayers often tend to be more "me-centered."

We need to ask the Lord for a Holy Audacity. Lord, help me to speak your Word with great boldness, and then lay my hands on the sick and let them be healed *in the name of Jesus.*

Now that's audacious!

Let the preceding verses be your own personal prayer today.

WEEK 9–TUESDAY

> ***"If the ax is dull and its edge unsharpened, more strength is needed but skill will bring success." Ecclesiastes 10:10 NIV84***

I'm sure that many of us were raised with knowing the importance of hard work, but sometimes God wants us to work smarter and not just harder. It's like using an ax that is dull to cut firewood—talk about hard work! But when that same ax is sharpened, the work becomes easier and more successful.

A church treasurer could keep admirable records by hand and then discover a software program that can do an even better job in far less time. Work smarter, not just harder.

Have you lost your edge? Has your spiritual impact become dull? Maybe it's time to go to the Lord and ask Him to restore your sharpened edge. Maybe your lack of success is not due to how hard you work but how smart. Is there a skill that you possess that needs to be improved?

When it comes to your spiritual witness, are you dull or sharp?

WEEK 9—WEDNESDAY

> *"Therefore confess your sins to each other and pray for each other so that you may be healed." James 5:16a NIV84*

I once sensed the need to schedule private meetings with individuals from our men's ministry. I had no agenda other than to connect with my brothers in a more confidential setting for about twenty to thirty minutes. Over the next few months I had fifteen private meetings with the men, and in most of those meetings, something special took place.

Over the course of sixty to ninety minutes, the men discovered a safe place where they became transparent and began confessing some very personal sins. Some of the men began to unburden themselves of stuff they had carried around for years, and healing took place.

Not everyone needs to know our business, but all of us need someone who we can confess our sins to. It doesn't have to be a pastor. It needs to be someone we trust with our confidential thoughts who is willing to love us, listen to us, and pray for us. Healing and freedom accompany confession.

Confession is good for the soul.

WEEK 9—THURSDAY

> *"But encourage one another daily, as long as it is called Today, so that none of you may be hardened by sin's deceitfulness." Hebrews 3:13 NIV84*

Many days I try to send out a note to whomever the Lord puts on my heart. In this era of texts, emails, and Instagram, there is something special about receiving a handwritten note in the mail. Simple things done in a simple way can bring some joy into someone else's life.

Encouraging others is something that needs to be part of our daily routine. God will bring you into contact with people today who will need to be built up. You don't need to be gifted or trained to encourage someone else. You just need to make a choice to show some kindness.

It is very easy for our hearts to become hardened by the cruel and fast-paced world we live in. One of the ways to keep our hearts soft is by reaching out to others. If you find yourself getting a bit self-absorbed lately, why not develop a habit of encouraging others?

Encourage one another* daily. *Do it every day!

WEEK 9–FRIDAY

> *"When the time drew near for David to die, he gave a charge to Solomon his son. 'I am about to go the way of all the earth,' he said. 'So be strong, show yourself a man.'" I Kings 2:1–2 NIV84*

David was giving some parting advice to his son, Solomon: "Show yourself a man." Men, it is not enough to merely call ourselves men; we have the responsibility to show ourselves to be men—men of God. It's time to man up.

God is not looking for men who merely show up for a worship service once in a while. He is looking for men who study the Word, pray, hang around other godly men, mentor other men, respect women, and assume the role as spiritual leader in their house.

Men, none of us are perfect, so we need to ask the Lord where we need to "man up." What are some godly habits that we can begin to develop? If you're a woman, thank a man who has shown himself to be a man.

Men are needy creatures and need to be told when we are doing something well.

Who is the most godly man you know?

Catching the Moments

What moments stand out to you from this past week?

What verse of Scripture was important to you during the past week?

In seven words or fewer, describe this past week.

_____

_____

_____

_____

_____

_____

_____

_____

_____

"Everything is permissible—but not everything is beneficial."
I Corinthians 10:23 NIV84

I am not a legalist. I believe it is permissible for some Christians to drink alcoholic beverages, but not me! You see, I am one of those people who is never satisfied with one drink. I always need more. So it is safer and wiser for me to have none. I don't have a problem if you have a glass of wine or a beer with your meal. I just think that we need to be more sensitive to our testimony than we do our freedom.

We should be more concerned with being a stumbling block to someone who has a drinking problem when we plan our cocktail hour at church events. I will not judge others for having that beer, but I believe the Church needs to exercise more caution in how we live our lives in public. We must not use our freedom to cause others to stumble.

Enjoy your freedom but not at the expense of someone else.

Are your actions causing someone else to stumble?

"Come." Matthew 14:29 NIV84

Peter was in a boat with the other disciples on a stormy sea at night and noticed that someone who looked like Jesus was walking on the water. Peter wanted to be sure, so he asked Jesus, "If it's you, tell me to come to you on the water." Jesus responded just by saying the word "Come."

With that, Peter stepped out of the boat and started walking on the water toward his Savior. Now we know what happened: Peter took his eyes off Jesus and began to sink, but Jesus reached out to save him. Then they walked on the water to get back into the boat.

Friends, there will be times in your life when Jesus is going to call you to get out of the boat and do the impossible: walk on water. Can that be scary? Yes. Will we make mistakes? Absolutely. Will Jesus be there to save you? All the time.

But once you have experienced walking on the water, the willingness to get out of the comfort of our boats becomes easier. Never easy but easier. Just keep your eyes on Jesus.

Can you identify a time when you "walked on water"?

WEEK 10—TUESDAY

> *"Simon Peter answered him, 'Lord, to whom shall we go? You have the words of eternal life. We have come to believe and to know that you are the Holy One of God.'" John 6:68–69 NIRV*

Jesus had just presented a hard teaching to His followers, which caused many of them to turn back and no longer follow Him. At this point Jesus turned to the Twelve Disciples He had chosen and asked them, "Do you want to leave too?"

Even though they were equally confused at this point, Peter said, "Lord, to whom shall we go? You have the words of eternal life."

What did Peter mean? I think he seemed to be implying: "Lord, even though we don't understand what's going on at the moment, we're not leaving. Where else are we going to go? We may not understand all Your words, but we know they all have eternal value. We're sticking with You."

We are not always going to understand everything that the Lord is teaching us, but don't leave Him. Where else are we going to go?

Stick with the Holy One of God!

"Speak up for those who cannot speak for themselves, for the rights of all who are destitute. Speak up and judge fairly; defend the rights of the poor and needy." Proverbs 31:8–9 NIV84

We have a responsibility as Christians to speak up for others. We all know what happens when good people keep silent. We are also told to judge others fairly. There are always those who say we are not supposed to judge others; that's not true—we are to judge fairly (the way we want others to judge us). And we are told to defend the rights of the poor and needy. We are to be people of action.

Here's the problem: sometimes we become so passionate about the cause that we lose our witness as Christians. There's nothing wrong with being passionate as long as the Holy Spirit is the source of our passion. Whether we are talking to someone about salvation or picketing with others about the rights of the poor, we still represent Jesus Christ. Be bold, be fair, and be just—you represent Jesus Christ.

God cares for the victim!

"You are not your own; you were bought at a price." I Corinthians 6:19–20 NIV84

A few years ago, they auctioned off some furniture that once belonged to President John F. Kennedy. One of the items on the auction block was a tiny stepstool (not much bigger than a car battery) that was worn, frayed, and ugly-looking, but it sold for more than $30,000. On its own, this little piece of furniture was worthless, but its value was determined by whom it belonged to: JFK.

There are far too many people who see themselves as worn, frayed, ugly-looking individuals who have no value. They devalue themselves because they compare themselves to other people. However, our value is not determined by who we are (in comparison to other people) but by whose we are (who we belong to). We were bought at a price: the blood of Jesus Christ on Calvary's cross.

Here is some even greater news: even if we should die, we do not lose our value because we still belong to the Lord. "So whether we live or die, we belong to the Lord." (Rom. 14:8)

Your life was so important to God that He was willing to sacrifice His only Son . . . for you!

WEEK 10—FRIDAY

"I commend to you our sister Phoebe, a servant of the church in Cenchrea." Romans 16:1 NIV84

At the conclusion of this incredible letter to the Roman Christians, the Apostle Paul mentions thirty-five people by name in the final chapter. The first one he mentions is Phoebe, who had been a great help to many people, including Paul. The apostle found it necessary to recognize individuals by name; so should we.

We all know that God knows and calls us by name; we are not a number to Him. We are not saved as a group; we are saved individually. What an honor to have such a relationship with our God for Him to call us by name. People like to be addressed by name.

I'm not always good with names, so that is why I work hard at remembering them as much as possible. Imagine how Phoebe must have felt when Paul commended her in his letter. Don't underestimate how others might feel when we commend them publicly. It makes them feel loved and recognized.

Look for an opportunity to commend someone else in front of others today.

Catching the Moments

What moments stand out to you from this past week?

What verse of Scripture was important to you during the past week?

In seven words or fewer, describe this past week.

_____

_____

_____

_____

_____

_____

_____

_____

_____

_____

WEEK 11–SUNDAY

"But we have this treasure in jars of clay to show that this all-surpassing power is from God and not from us." 2 Corinthians 4:7 NIV84

Even though I am just an earthen jar of clay, God designed me to be filled with heavenly contents. I am so glad that is how I am put together. Occasionally I forget and begin to think that this jar of clay is "hot stuff." However, God, in His mercy, quickly helps me put things in perspective. He wants others to discover the treasure that I have inside of me, and so He sometimes allows this jar to be broken and reveal my heavenly contents. Other times, when I realize how blessed I am, He allows it to just overflow in my life and spill into the lives of others.

Don't be overly impressed with yourself. Even though you were made by God, you are most effective in His kingdom when others don't notice you. You are not the treasure; you are a treasure chest.

Thank You, Lord, for being such a good Potter.

I've got some all-surpassing power ready to break loose in me. Hallelujah!

WEEK 11–MONDAY

"I have told you this so that my joy may be in you and that your joy may be complete." John 15:11 NIV84

One of the first things I look for when I walk into a new congregation is *joy*. Not mere happiness shown with a hearty handshake and an invitation to sign the guestbook but real joy in the Lord, where the Spirit of God has transformed people into a new creation.

Happiness usually comes from the external circumstances around us. When I get that raise or am affirmed publicly by someone else, it makes me happy. Happiness is good, but it doesn't last. Real joy—God-given joy—comes from within. When things are not falling into place around me, I can still have joy, because my joy is not found in my circumstances but in the Lord. Only Jesus can give you that.

Occasionally we lose our joy, but the Good News is that we can pray like David: "Restore to me the joy of your salvation." (Ps. 51:12). Jesus did not come so that we could have some joy; He wanted our joy to be complete.

Would other friends describe you as a joyful person?

WEEK 11—TUESDAY

"They will act religious, but they will reject the power that could make them godly." 2 Timothy 3:5 NLT

Paul was talking about the marks of the last days. One of those marks will be deceptive religious people who hold to a mere form of godliness. What is the power that makes us godly? The power of the Holy Spirit within us! Acting religious requires prideful knowledge; living godly requires humble surrender.

As much as I may preach against it, I still have that hidden desire to occasionally appear very religious to other people. Our "old man" loves to appear righteous to others, but our "new man" loves to seek the righteousness of our God. A true follower of Jesus wants to live a godly life but recognizes that we can't live such a life in our own power. We need the power of the Holy Spirit.

Jesus didn't teach His disciples how to act right; He taught them how to be godly. In these last days, we need more godly people and fewer religious people.

Don't reject the power that is so personal and real.

WEEK 11—WEDNESDAY

"Grace and truth came through Jesus Christ." John 1:17 NIV84

The Church is not perfect. All of us who are members of the Body of Christ still have our issues. Nonetheless, isn't it amazing how people are still being drawn to the Church? What is it that draws the unsaved to an imperfect group of people? It is God's grace! The world is hungry for grace, that undeserved and uncompromised love of God that seeks nothing but the best for whomever it touches. There are so many people who long for genuine love and truth and will always pause when they are in an atmosphere of grace.

Grace is unique to Christianity. All other religions expect us to follow certain rules and regulations in order for us to come to God's level. But our God loved us so much that He came down to us and extended to us *grace* through His Son, Jesus Christ. Grace can make an imperfect Church attractive to hurting people.

I love the acronym of GRACE that explains it so well: God's Riches At Christ's Expense.

May God's grace make your life more appealing to others.

WEEK 11—THURSDAY

"Get Mark and bring him with you, because he is helpful to me in my ministry." 2 Timothy 4:11 NIV84

Mark was someone who deserted Paul and Barnabas on a missionary journey. Barnabas wanted to give him a second chance on a future mission trip, but Paul did not agree. Their disagreement was so intense that it caused Paul and Barnabas to split up. All over Mark!

Years later, the Lord not only changed Mark but also changed Paul. Paul tells Timothy to bring Mark with him, "because he is very helpful to me in my ministry." The deserter had become a helper. Isn't our God incredible?

I think back and remember so many people who were helpful to me in my ministry. They made my job so much easier. Where would we be without all the helpers God has placed in our lives?

Who has been helpful to you? Who are those people God has raised up to come alongside you and assist you in your ministry? Don't take these people for granted.

Acknowledge those who have been helpful. Affirm them and accept them.

WEEK 11—FRIDAY

> *"But if we hope for what we do not yet have, we wait for it patiently." Romans 8:25 NIV84*

Please pay attention to those words: "We hope…we wait." And inserted between those words are "for what we do not yet have." Heaven has to be at the top of our list, but there are plenty of earthly needs that keep us hoping and waiting.

Lord, for that loved one who keeps on rebelling against You, I hope and I wait for Your answer. For that depression that has invaded my soul, I hope and I wait. For the loneliness that keeps me in the dark, I hope and I wait. For the physical ailment that continues to torment me, I hope and I wait.

Keep on hoping and waiting for those things that we do not yet have. One day we will have them. Your hoping and your waiting is not in vain. Don't ever give up on the things that God has promised. Ask the Lord to teach you how to hope and wait with a holy expectation. One day…

WAIT—Why Am I Troubled?

Catching the Moments

What moments stand out to you from this past week?

What verse of Scripture was important to you during the past week?

In seven words or fewer, describe this past week.

_____

_____

_____

_____

_____

_____

_____

_____

_____

_____

_____

_____

WEEK 12–SUNDAY

"And I tell you that you are Peter, and on this rock I will build my church, and the gates of Hades will not overcome it." Matthew 16:18 NIV84

Peter had just boldly declared who Jesus Christ was in his life: "You are the Messiah, the Son of the living God." (v. 16). God longs to reveal His Son to people whose hearts are open and teachable.

When Jesus said, "And on this rock I will build my church," he did not mean he was building the church upon Peter. Jesus was going to build His church upon people who had received a revelation from God Himself that Jesus was the Messiah, the Son of the Living God. Satan will never prevail against the Church that has received such a revelation.

Have you received that revelation yet, or are you merely repeating what everyone is saying?

*Always remember that Jesus said, "This is **my** church." It's not ours; it is His.*

WEEK 12–MONDAY

"And let our people also learn to maintain good works, to meet urgent needs, that they may not be unfruitful." Titus 3:14 NKJV

Don't stop performing good works in the name of Jesus. It is what God expects from us. We are not saved *by* our good works, but we are certainly saved *for* good works. Keep on doing good, my friends.

God wants His people to be prepared to meet urgent needs. God may just have positioned you and equipped you to meet an important need that will leave a lasting effect in someone else's life. You may be the one whom Jesus has chosen to meet an urgent need today.

God has called us to be fruitful. Jesus said in John 15:16, "I chose you and appointed you so that you might go and bear fruit—fruit that will last." Don't be unfruitful—bear some fruit that gives glory to our Lord and Savior.

Be ready to step outside the shell in which we live in order to represent our God in a powerful way.

WEEK 12–TUESDAY

"But just as he who called you is holy, so be holy in all you do."
I Peter 1:15 NIV84

Are you normal? Your response will be measured by whose standard you are using. The definition of the word "normal" is: "conforming to a standard; usual; typical, or expected." What is the standard you are using to define normalcy? If we are honest, there will always be times we will appear to be normal to some and other times we will seem abnormal.

God's standard is one of holiness. That is the "norm" He has set for our lives. But wait! It's impossible for me to always live up to such a standard, because I still deal with this problem called "sin." I always seem to fall short of His holy standard—that's normal. But thank God that I can confess my sins and receive forgiveness because of the blood of my Savior. That's normal.

When we live our lives according to what God expects of us, we can still appear abnormal to those who are not believers. Even some marginal believers will think we're a bit odd.

"My God, my God, why have you forsaken me?" Matthew 27:46 NIV84

During Jesus's earthly ministry, He always referred to the First Person of the Trinity as "Father." Only once did He refer to Him as "God"— that was when He hung on the cross bearing the sin of the whole world. As He experienced that "sin" separation on our behalf, He needed the divine nature of His God. All the other times He was calling out to and staying connected to His Father. Jesus—the Son of God and the Son of Man!

As God's children, there are times we need to connect with our Divine God and other times we need to connect with our Father. In our daily walk, we need to connect with our Spiritual Daddy just like Jesus did. Jesus said that He only spoke and did what His Father instructed Him to do. When He taught us to pray, He said we should pray, "Our Father." But when it comes to *sin*, that's when we need to call out to "Our God."

Praise to "The God and Father of the Lord Jesus." 2 Corinthians 11:31

"But because my servant Caleb has a different spirit and follows me wholeheartedly, I will bring him into the land he went to, and his descendents will inherit it." Numbers 14:24 NIV84

The spies came back with a fearful and negative report after checking out the Promised Land that the Lord had sworn to give them. They were afraid of the giants who stood in their way. Caleb was different. He saw the same giants but believed that their God was bigger. It is not always easy being different.

If you are following Jesus Christ wholeheartedly, there will be times you must be willing to stand alone and be different. Not everyone will always agree with you. I know plenty of Christians who could easily be described as different, but when urgent prayer is needed, they are usually the first ones called upon.

Don't set out to merely be different. Make it your goal to follow the Lord and trust the Lord wholeheartedly, even when others don't. The Lord's blessing belongs to those who are ready to believe His promises.

Don't be afraid of being different; be afraid of being the same as everyone else.

WEEK 12—FRIDAY

> *"Israel's leaders took charge, and the people gladly followed. Praise the Lord!" Judges 5:2 (NLT)*

The Church needs more leaders led by the Spirit who rise up and take charge. Not those who dominate the people and lord over them with power. They don't need leaders who "wing it" and merely do maintenance work. People will gladly follow leaders who are following Jesus. Sheep need shepherds whom they can trust. Thank God for leaders who lead and followers who follow. Praise the Lord!

The Church needs more shepherds and fewer cowboys. Sheep will naturally follow a shepherd. When cowboys want to move cattle, they will get behind them and drive them to the desired location. You can't drive sheep because they will scatter. You've got to lead them.

If your congregation is finding it difficult to recruit volunteers, maybe (not always) the problem lies in the leaders. What is your role in the Church? Are you taking charge and leading others in a way that would be pleasing to the Lord?

If your role is to lead, take charge. Gladly follow those who do.
Praise the Lord!

Catching the Moments

What moments stand out to you from this past week?

What verse of Scripture was important to you during the past week?

In seven words or fewer, describe this past week.

_____

_____

_____

_____

_____

_____

_____

_____

_____

_____

_____

> *"Then Jesus looked up and said, 'Father, I thank you that you have heard me.'" John 11:42 NIV84*

Jesus was about to raise Lazarus from the dead. In minutes a man wrapped in his grave clothes was going to walk out of the tomb. Please notice that Jesus was thanking His Father before the miracle occurred. Jesus knew that His Father had heard Him. In fact, in the next verse Jesus even went as far as to say, "I knew that you always hear me." If it were me, I might have waited to thank the Lord after He had answered my prayer.

We need to remember this principle in our own prayer life. Whenever we are in need of a miracle, or just an answer to a prayer, start thanking the Lord that He has heard you. When you are praying for your needs, when you have finished, tell the Lord, "Thank You that You have heard me." When you are praying for someone else, when you have finished, say, "Thank You that You have heard me."

When you ask something that is humanly impossible, say, "Thank You, Lord, that You have heard me."

WEEK 13—MONDAY

> *"Jesus found a young donkey and sat on it." John 12:14 NIRV*

As you look at Jesus's triumphant entry into Jerusalem, may you try to find yourself in the story. Who do you identify with? Take your time to read each of the Gospel writers' account, and pay attention to all the characters involved. There are so many wonderful truths and teaching points that can be found.

Who do I identify with? I've often identified my role in the ministry like that of the donkey. That lowly donkey had the responsibility of lifting up Jesus and carrying Him a little further down the road into the lives of other people. We have a tendency to overcomplicate ministry, but when you think of it from the donkey's point of view, it is something that we can do.

If God could speak to Balaam through a donkey, then he can use me to lift up Jesus and carry Him a little further down the road. I can be stubborn at times, but nonetheless, the Lord needs donkeys like us.

May you intentionally lift up Jesus and carry Him when you leave the house.

WEEK 13—TUESDAY

> *"As they pass through the Valley of Baka, they make it a place of springs; the autumn rains also cover it with pools." Psalm 84:6 NIV84*

The word "Baka" can be translated into the word "weeping." We will all have our valleys of weeping, but the key is to keep passing through them. Don't stop, don't lie down; keep moving forward because there will be an end to your weeping. "Yea, though I walk *through* the valley of the shadow of death . . ." (Ps. 23). The word "pools" can be translated into "blessings." If we keep walking by faith and passing through our valley of weeping, the Lord can actually cover that place with blessings.

God is fully aware of those prolonged times of weeping. He loves you deeply and wants to use this difficult moment in your life to glorify Himself. It is absolutely incredible how He can turn weeping into laughing, mourning into dancing, and despair into hope. He wants to cover you with His blessings.

Keep walking through your valley! Don't try and understand it all; just keep walking.

WEEK 13—WEDNESDAY

"At that moment the curtain of the temple was torn in two from the top to bottom." Matthew 27:51 NIV84

The moment that Jesus Christ died on the cross, our Heavenly Father sent an incredible message to the world. The veil in the temple was torn in two. Up until that point, the awesome presence of God hid behind that curtain. Only the high priest on the Day of Atonement was allowed to enter the Holy of Holies on behalf of the sins of mankind. Our High Priest, Jesus Christ, had now torn that separating curtain in two and given mankind access to God.

All that was needed for the atonement of our sins was now finished. Our God seemed to be saying, "Now you can come to Me on your own. You don't have to let the high priest do it for you."

What a moment! I can't imagine what kind of activity was taking place in heaven. We only got to see the torn curtain on earth; heaven knew the meaning behind it all.

It truly was a Good Friday!

WEEK 13—THURSDAY

"Now that I, your Lord and Teacher, have washed your feet, you also should wash one another's feet." John 13:14 NIV84

Hours before Jesus was to be arrested, He humbled Himself to do something only servants were supposed to do: wash feet. It was such a humiliating task that Peter initially would not even allow Jesus to wash his, but Jesus was about to teach His disciples a valuable lesson.

On Maundy Thursday some churches will have foot-washing ceremonies incorporated into their worship services. There are some important things to be learned from this humble example, but sometimes we miss the point. We need fewer foot-washing ceremonies in the Church and more people who are willing to set aside their pride and serve others in humbling ways. "Do not be proud, but be willing to associate with people of low position. Do not be conceited." (Rom. 12:16)

Rather than wash your friend's feet in church, why not give up your shoes to someone on your way to work . . . and then pray for them?

Jesus did not come to be served but to serve and give His life as a ransom for many. Go and do likewise.

WEEK 13–FRIDAY

"When they had sung a hymn, they went out to the Mount of Olives." Matthew 26:30 NIV84

At the conclusion of the Last Supper, Jesus and His disciples sang a hymn. Can you image what that had to be like? Singing a hymn with the Messiah! Wow! Talk about a worship experience! What was it like to watch Jesus sing a hymn? Did they sing a Passover hymn? Who led the singing? Was the hymn they sang one of public domain (just kidding)?

Can you imagine Peter saying, "I don't like that hymn. Let's sing another one." I doubt if Thomas complained about the worship style or that John was singing offkey. They had no keyboard, organ, hymnbooks, or overhead screens.

The next time you are in a worship setting, try and put into perspective what worship is all about. Jesus took time to sing a hymn before leaving the upper room to be arrested.

"God is spirit, and his worshipers must worship in the Spirit and in truth." (John 4:24)

Worship: it's all about Him!

Catching the Moments

What moments stand out to you from this past week?

What verse of Scripture was important to you during the past week?

In seven words or fewer, describe this past week.

_____

_____

_____

_____

_____

_____

_____

_____

_____

_____

_____

_____

WEEK 14–SUNDAY

> *"I died, but see, I am alive forevermore, and I have the keys of (absolute control and victory over) death and Hades (the realm of the dead)." Revelation 1:18 AMP*

The resurrection of Jesus Christ is not just some nice story that fills the books of Scripture. When He rose, He held the keys of absolute control and victory over sin, death, and the devil. If I serve such a sovereign and powerful Savior, and He holds the keys to my future, why do I allow myself to be influenced by my "defeated foes"?

When the fear of death begins to invade our thinking, we need to remind ourselves that our Savior has absolute control over death. When Satan begins to fill our minds with doubt and desperation, we need to remind him that he's already defeated.

The resurrection of Jesus changed the course of history. Because He lives, I can face tomorrow. My soul is excited that my Victorious King has everything under control.

Thank You, Jesus, that you hold the keys!

WEEK 14–MONDAY

> *"If there is no resurrection of the dead, then not even Christ has been raised. And if Christ has not been raised, our preaching is useless and so is your faith." I Corinthians 15:13–14 NIV84*

If Christ were not raised from the dead, I wouldn't have the hope of seeing my mom and dad again.

If Christ were not raised from the dead, I would not be in the profession I am.

If Christ were not raised from the dead, fear of my future would have been too much for me to bear.

If Christ were not raised from the dead, I would still be carrying the heavy load of my own sinfulness.

If Christ were not raised from the dead, I would be a pathetic basketcase.

If Christ were not raised from the dead, I would not have heaven to look forward to.

But Jesus was raised. And His victory has become my victory, and my faith is not useless.

My spirit is filled with hope and my future is secure. Because He lives, I can face tomorrow.

Christ has risen! Alleluia!

WEEK 14—TUESDAY

> ***"When I see the blood, I will pass over you." Exodus 12:13 NIV84***

What an incredible night that had to be in Egypt. As the blood of the Passover Lamb was applied to the doorposts of their own houses, the Israelites were passed over by the angel of death. The blood of that precious, spotless lamb is the only thing that would save them. That Passover Lamb is a wonderful picture of our Passover Lamb, Jesus Christ. I am not saved by having my name on a church roster or being able to recite the Ten Commandments. I am saved because the blood of Jesus Christ has been applied to the doorpost of my heart.

I am a sinner saved by grace. I still have my issues and have my moments of rebellion. But when my Loving Father sees the blood of Christ applied to the doorposts of my heart, the punishment that I deserve passes over me.

God said, "When I see the blood!" Does He see the blood of Christ applied to the doorposts of your heart?

We Thank God for Passover!

WEEK 14—WEDNESDAY

> *"The Lord directs the steps of the godly. He delights in every detail of their lives." Psalm 37:23 NLT*

The Lord not only points us in the right direction; He even wants to direct each step we take. He doesn't want to control each of our steps, He wants to direct them. There's a difference. He just loves it when we want Him involved in every one of our steps. He finds delight in every step we take and at times wants us to pay close attention to the details along the way.

He not only wants to direct the steps of the godly; He wants to direct the stops of the godly. He tells us where to step and tells us when to stop. If we interpreted this literally, it would take us a really long time to reach our destination. The thing to remember is when we strive to live a godly life, God will direct our steps and our stops. It is a matter of trust.

The Lord is actually delighted when I allow Him to direct my steps.

WEEK 14—THURSDAY

> *"So then, just as you received Christ Jesus as Lord, continue to live your lives in him, rooted and built up in him." Colossians 2:6–7 NIRV*

Spiritual growth is a process. It can occasionally be painful, scary, and humbling, but it is always worth it. It takes time for our roots to grow down deep into Jesus. Sometimes the Lord will even repot us because our roots need more room to grow. If we stay where we are, we may not grow and blossom, so God, in His mercy, decides to repot us.

When that happens, I've been known to resist because I like the pot I'm in right now. It's comfortable where I'm at, and I would prefer to just stay put in my pot. But Jesus reassures me that in order for me to grow, I need to be in a place where my spiritual roots can extend out further. When I finally say yes and surrender to His will, I am always built up and edified.

Stay rooted in Jesus and not your "comfort zones."

WEEK 14–FRIDAY

> *"Has the Lord redeemed you? Then speak out! Tell others he has redeemed you from your enemies." Psalm 107:2 NLT*

This psalm tells us that if we have been redeemed by the Lord, we need to speak it out and tell others. If we are not speaking out, maybe it's because we've forgotten what it is like to be redeemed. One of the definitions of "redeemed" is "to free from captivity by payment of ransom." Jesus Christ has paid the ransom of His own life so that we could be set free from the enemies of sin, death, and the devil. If it weren't for the ransom paid by His blood, we would all spend eternity separated from God in the depths and suffering of hell.

Let the redeemed of the Lord say so. If someone asks you why you are so joyful, be prepared to tell them, "I've been redeemed!" Who knows where the conversation will go from there!

Has the Lord redeemed you? If you've never done it before, why not ask Jesus to come into your heart and experience the redemption He has purchased just for you.

Be prepared to "speak it out" to someone today!

Catching the Moments

What moments stand out to you from this past week?

What verse of Scripture was important to you during the past week?

In seven words or fewer, describe this past week.

_____

_____

_____

_____

_____

_____

_____

_____

_____

_____

_____

_____

"Finally, brothers, whatever is true, whatever is noble, whatever is right, whatever is pure, whatever is lovely, whatever is admirable—if anything is excellent or praiseworthy—think about such things." Philippians 4:8 NIV84

How good are you at "thought management"? I'm much better at time management than I am at thought management, but I'm getting better. To manage my time is a good thing, because it makes my day far more effective and productive. Imagine if we learn how to manage our thoughts with the same diligence.

What do you think about? Our thought life has a lot to do with defining our identity. In Proverbs we are told that as a man thinketh, so is he (Prov. 23:7). Paul told the Philippians to think about things that are excellent and praiseworthy. We have been given the power and authority to take captive those thoughts that are contrary to the Word of God (2 Cor. 10:5). Ask the Lord to help you with your thought management today. It will definitely make a difference in your day. Don't let Satan control your thought life.

Let the Spirit of the Lord change the way you think.

"When the Lord saw that he had gone over to look, God called to him from within the bush, 'Moses! Moses!' And Moses said, 'Here I am.'" Exodus 3:4 NIV84

Moses was out tending a flock of sheep when he noticed a bush that didn't burn up. He was curious and decided to check out this strange sight. It was then that God spoke to him from within the bush. God spoke to Moses on an ordinary day while he was performing an ordinary task.

It's not every day that we have a "burning bush" moment with God, but when they do occur, it's usually during an ordinary moment. Yes, He still speaks to us during an anointed worship time with other Christians. Yes, He still speaks to us during our morning devotions. But He also speaks to us while we are doing the laundry, riding a bus, doing a spreadsheet at work, and mowing the lawn. Just keep your eyes and ears open. There may be a burning bush hidden in the normal routine of your day.

God is able to use our curiosity for His purpose.

WEEK 15—TUESDAY

"You have set our iniquities before you, our secret sins in the light of your presence." Psalm 90:8 NIV84

Mark Twain once said, "Everyone is a moon, and has a dark side which he never shows to anybody." Think about that! Do you have a dark side? Do you have some sins hidden way back in a closet in your heart that no one knows about? I can't speak for you, but I've had some dark sides that I had very neatly locked away so that no one else would ever know . . . except God.

When our "dark side" is exposed by God's light, we've got choices to make. Am I going to let this hidden sin keep me captive forever, or am I going to confess and be rid of it? It was a great day when I finally realized that Jesus accepts me—even with my dark side. When we allow Christ to be Lord of our lives, our dark side can no longer hold us hostage.

The power of the cross is greater than the darkest of our sins.

WEEK 15—WEDNESDAY

> *"You will fill me with joy in your presence, with eternal pleasures at your right hand." Psalm 16:11 NIV84*

A recent statistic revealed that more than 30 percent of those who attend church have never felt God's presence during the worship service. I know what some will say: "We are not saved by how we feel; we walk by faith, not by how we feel. God's existence is not based on our feeling it." No argument from me.

Nonetheless, we are told that we will be filled with joy in the Lord's presence. How can we not occasionally experience God's presence? He longs for us to experience His joy, peace, comfort, deliverance, healing, and love. Those are characteristics that are part of God's nature that are intended to occasionally be felt.

I think that some people are afraid of feeling God's presence. That's not wrong. Ask Moses when he was talking with the Burning Bush. Ask Isaiah as he watched the angels singing "Holy, holy, holy." Ask John when he saw Jesus in the book of Revelation.

When we get to heaven, we will feel God's presence forever. Why not enjoy it now?

WEEK 15—THURSDAY

> *"I have brought you glory on earth by finishing the work you gave me to do." John 17:4 NIV84*

Jesus had come into this world to show and demonstrate the love of God to a broken world. He had done everything His Father had asked Him to do. He had loved the unlovable, healed the sick, raised the dead, and showed the power and love of God in everyday life. He had finished all that needed to be done—up until that point. But if He had stopped short of the cross, God's love would not have been complete.

The ultimate display of God's love was about to be shown to all in heaven and on earth.

Have you finished all that God has asked you to do? He wants us to finish well. Don't leave unfinished those things that are in our power to complete. Take care of those things that have been sitting in your "unfinished business" box. Don't stop short!

We bring God glory when we finish the work that He gives us to do.

WEEK 15–FRIDAY

"For God did not give us a spirit of timidity, but a spirit of power, of love, and of self-discipline." 2 Timothy 1:7 NIV84

Brothers and sisters in Christ, *it is not a time to be timid.* We live in a society where we are beaten down and beaten up. We trust in the promises of man more than we do the promises of God. As Christians we have become so careful that we are starting to lose the power of our witness.

As a believer in Jesus Christ, I have been given a spirit of power. I am promised that I am able to boldly witness my Christian faith and pray for people in need. I have been given a Spirit of love. That means I am able to love others the same way Jesus did. I have been given a Spirit of self-discipline. As I surrender my life to the Holy Spirit, He is able to bring control and discipline into my chaotic life.

Join with me as we declare that **it is not time to be timid.** *I am a follower of Jesus Christ.*

Catching the Moments

What moments stand out to you from this past week?

What verse of Scripture was important to you during the past week?

In seven words or fewer, describe this past week.

_____

_____

_____

_____

_____

_____

_____

_____

_____

_____

_____

_____

"Now faith is confidence in what we hope for and assurance about what we do not see. This is what the ancients were commended for." Hebrews 11:1–2 NIRV

Chapter eleven of Hebrews has been defined by some as the Hall of Fame of Faith. It lists many people who lived by faith.

By faith Abel brought God a better offering than Cain did. By faith Enoch . . . By faith Noah . . . By faith Abraham . . . By faith Sarah . . . By faith Isaac . . . By faith Jacob . . . By faith Joseph . . . By faith Moses . . . By faith Rahab . . . By faith Steve . . . By faith (fill in the blank) . . . Do you get it?

When we walk and live by faith, God will commend us for it. Without faith it is impossible to please God, but He rewards those who seek Him—by faith (see Hebrews 11:6).

People who walk by faith have an assurance that God will do what He has promised.

Where does such faith come from? It comes from the Word of God (Rom. 10:17).

Don't just read the Word; trust the Word and live the Word.

"If you are willing and obedient, you will eat the good things of the land." Isaiah 1:19 NIRV

We all long to feast upon the abundance of God's blessings. The key is to give special attention to the words "willing" and "obedient."

God longs for us to respond to Him with love and not out of fear. He does not want our relationship to be Him pulling the strings of His puppets. Willingness is something He loves. If we are submissive in our heart to the Lord's command, He has promised to bless us. Not because we deserve it or because we are willing enough but because He is just a God who loves to bless His children. Obedience shows that we are resolved to do it God's way. Jesus said, "If anyone loves me, he will obey my teaching." (John 14:23)

When you are truly in love with someone, you are willing and obedient to please them. There are rewards that truly follow our obedience.

Oh, taste and see that the Lord is good, and that He gives us good things to eat and enjoy.

WEEK 16–TUESDAY

"And free those who all their lives were held in slavery by their fear of death." Hebrews 2:15 NIV84

If we are honest with ourselves, all of us deal with a certain amount of fear when it comes to our death. Even though I have an assurance of my eternal home in heaven through my faith in Jesus Christ, I still wonder when and how I will die. You see, I don't fear what will happen to me when I die; it's the process leading up to death that I still wonder about. Will it be painful? Will my loved ones be cared for? Those questions and others still pop into my mind from time to time.

While I still deal with some of those fears, I am no longer a slave of those fears. Jesus Christ has not only freed me from the fear of death, but He has also freed me from the fear of how I will die. God has destined me to spend eternity with Him in heaven. His love for me is casting out the fear I have about death.

If you have any fear of death, talk to God about it. After all, He already knows.

WEEK 16—WEDNESDAY

"But in the seventh year the land is to have a sabbath of rest, a sabbath to the Lord. Do not sow your fields or prune your vineyards." Leviticus 25:4 NIV84

I spend a couple summers of my life working on a farm in Pennsylvania. The farmer I worked for was an incredible man of God. He believed in putting the Lord first, not only in his personal life but also in his work. When I questioned him once as to why he was not using a certain field to produce more crops, he said he was giving the land a rest. Every several years he rested some land in order that it would become more productive the following year. While surrounding farmers got a good harvest, he got a bumper one.

God has told us to observe His Sabbath. He wants us to remain rested and strong so that we can continue to produce a bumper crop in our personal life. Take time to rest, my friend. If you do, your productivity will increase.

There are no exceptions to the rule.

WEEK 16—THURSDAY

"When your words came, I ate them; they were my joy and my heart's delight." Jeremiah 15:16 NIV84

I can't imagine what my life would be like without my Bible. I am given so much joy and comfort every morning as I feed on the wonderful truths found in it as I sit in my recliner with a cup of coffee. You get used to your own personal Bible—the highlighted passages, the notes written in the margin, and all the little symbols that only have meaning for me. One Bible usually lasts me about a decade before it starts to fall apart, but I've saved every worn-out Bible from the past. They stir up certain memories that I will take to heaven with me. It is truly sad that so many Bibles never become personal property of their owners but remain on the shelves, collecting dust.

Meanwhile, on the other side of the world, Christians suffer simply because they own a Bible. They don't get to sit in their recliner with a cup of coffee and enjoy the inspired Word of God. They sit in a jail with the memory of what was planted in their heart.

Feast on God's Word.

WEEK 16—FRIDAY

> *"Let us come before him with thanksgiving and extol him with music and song." Psalm 95:2 NIV84*

I love music and song. It is truly a gift of God. I even love some of those Rock 'n' roll songs that I grew up with in the 1960s and '70s. But there are certain hymns and praise choruses that have found a very special place in my heart. "Be Still My Soul," "In the Garden," and "We Shall Overcome" are hymns I always enjoy singing. "It Is Well with My Soul" always brings me back to my mom's funeral. Praise choruses such as "Shout to the Lord" and "These Are the Days of Elijah" will always be some of my *oldies but goodies*.

Scripture clearly tells us that there will be music and singing in heaven. I can't even imagine what it will be like to sing "Holy Holy Holy" with the countless angels around the throne of God. If you happen to be standing next to me when that moment comes, you will be equally overcome with emotion as I know I will be.

Spend some time today lifting up the Lord with music and song.

Catching the Moments

What moments stand out to you from this past week?

What verse of Scripture was important to you during the past week?

In seven words or fewer, describe this past week.

_____

_____

_____

_____

_____

_____

_____

_____

_____

_____

_____

_____

_____

_____

"Those who carried materials did their work with one hand and held a weapon in the other, and each of the builders wore his sword at his side as he worked." Nehemiah 4:17–18 NIV84

Building the wall around Jerusalem required work and a weapon. Even though there was opposition, they continued their labor as they carried a weapon. That means that they trusted God as they worked and were also alert to what the enemy was doing.

Satan is always working to discourage us in kingdom building, but we must not let his opposition stop us. Keep serving, keep teaching, keep singing, keep doing what you are doing, but pay attention. Always be armed with the Word of God to use against him as needed.

You need to arm yourself with God's Word every morning before you leave the house, and then wear it as your sword throughout the day. Hard work will not prevent Satan from attacking you, but the Word will defend you. God needs more laborers in His kingdom, but He wants us to be spiritually alert.

One of Satan's greatest weapons is man's ignorance of God's Word.

WEEK 17–MONDAY

"In the beginning God created . . ." Genesis 1:1 NIV84

Our God is creative; that is an understatement! He created the heavens and the earth, every solar system, musical major and minor tones, the human cell, the human brain, etc. He created things out of nothing with a mere word. He spoke, and His creative powers were put into practice.

He created us. Because we are created in His image, we also have the ability to be creative. We need to ask the Lord to stir up those gifts that He has placed within us. I think the Church should be blazing the path of creative ideas because we have been endowed with a spirit of creativity.

I pray that some of the Lord's original thoughts find their way into your thinking. Write a book, paint a picture, solve a problem, discover the cure for cancer, do something that no one else is doing; *be creative*!

I know the Bible teaches that God's thoughts are not our thoughts (Isaiah 55:8), but He is more than able to pass a few of those along to us.

WEEK 17- TUESDAY

"When these things begin to take place, stand up and lift up your heads, because your redemption is drawing near." Luke 21:28 NIV84

We are in the last days. I say that with a strong sense of certainty. I don't know when Jesus is coming back, but the signs of the times are certainly sending a strong message that we are close. Rather than being worried and upset over all the difficult times that will precede our Lord's Second Coming, Jesus gives us some wonderful advice. We are not to hang our heads and cower in fear; we are told to stand up, lift up our heads, and be excited because that day is very near.

It's hard to imagine what that day will be like, but I am absolutely sure that as believers in Jesus Christ, we will not be disappointed. Don't be afraid of the wars and rumors of wars that are taking place around the world. Our Savior, Jesus Christ, is greater than any nation or world leader. Stand to your feet, Church. The time is close.

The Second Coming of Jesus is not "doomsday" preaching. It's our redemption drawing near.

WEEK 17–WEDNESDAY

"Let no one be found among you who . . . practices divination or sorcery, interprets omens, engages in witchcraft, or cast spells, or who is a medium or spiritist or who consults the dead." Deuteronomy 18:10–11 NIV84

Don't play games with the occult! Many see dabbling in the spiritual realm as just fun and games: *What's the big deal of playing with a Ouija board? I just follow my astrological sign for fun. What harm is there is seeking the guidance of a spiritual reader?*

In the preceding verse, God was talking to the children Israel right before they were to enter the Promised Land. He was warning them not to get involved in any practices that were detestable to Him. There is a real spiritual realm around us that we cannot see but is very powerful. We may begin our involvement in occult activity innocently enough, but it doesn't take much for Satan to get you more involved. Just as God and His holy angels are real, so are the devil and his destructive demons. While I firmly believe that followers of Jesus cannot be possessed, we can certainly be oppressed.

Seek God for your guidance and direction.

WEEK 17–THURSDAY

"The man brought me back to the entrance to the temple, and I saw water coming out from under the threshold of the temple toward the east." Ezekiel 47:1 NIV84

Ezekiel 47 is a beautiful chapter that talks about the river flowing from the temple. It says that "where the river flows everything will live." (v. 9). This river of life and healing speaks to me about the power of the Holy Spirit in our lives, where "rivers of living water will flow from within us." (John 7:38)

Some venture into this river and only stay on the edge where it is only ankle-deep (v. 3). Others go further where it is knee-deep (v. 4), waist-deep (v. 4), and some to the place where it is deep enough to swim (v. 5). It is a shame that some people stay in the shallow end of their relationship with God while others explore the depths where the Holy Spirit allows them to flow.

Don't be afraid to go into the deep end of your relationship with God. You will have to trust the Holy Spirit to take you where He wants you to be, but you will not be disappointed.

Lord, teach me how to swim (v. 5).

WEEK 17—FRIDAY

> *"My sacrifice, O God, is a broken spirit; a broken and contrite heart you, God, will not despise." Psalm 51:17 NIRV*

What is a broken and contrite heart? It is a heart that is hurting and in need of God's healing. It is a heart that knows it deserves little but has been given much. It is a heart that knows it has sinned against God but knows that it is also loved by God. It is a heart that is truly sorry yet at the same time knows it is truly loved by God. It is a heart that knows who we are but also knows who God is.

When you really think about it, when we have a broken and contrite heart, we are closer to God than we realize. David also said in Psalm 34:18, "The Lord is close to the brokenhearted and saves those who are crushed in spirit."

Our God is full of grace and mercy and longs to be close to us—especially when we need it the most.

If all you have to offer to God is a broken and contrite spirit today, He is glad to receive your precious gift.

Catching the Moments

What moments stand out to you from this past week?

What verse of Scripture was important to you during the past week?

In seven words or fewer, describe this past week.

_____

_____

_____

_____

_____

_____

_____

_____

_____

_____

_____

_____

WEEK 18—SUNDAY

"What, then, shall we say in response to these things? If God is for us, who can be against us? He who did not spare his own son, but gave him up for us all—how will he not also, along with him, graciously give us all things?" Romans 8:31–32 NIRV

How secure are you in your relationship with the Lord? Are you confident that He really loves you and will take care of you? Look at Romans 8:31–32 again and insert your personal name in the blank spaces. If fact, read the verse out loud:"If God is for _____, who can be against _____? He who did not spare his own son, but gave him up for _____— how will he not also, along with him, graciously give _____ all things?"

We need to accept the fact that God is for us and not against us. Some of us may have been raised with the lie that God is for some people and against others. Jesus really loves *you*, and He wants to graciously give to you all that you need.

Say out loud, "God is for me."

WEEK 18—MONDAY

"Therefore he is able to save completely those who come to God through him, because he always lives to intercede for them." Hebrews 7:25 NIV84

Jesus did not die on the cross and sacrifice His life so that we could be partially saved. When we are saved, we are saved *completely*. Spiritual maturity is a process, but our salvation is not.

Years ago, I had a chat with one of our members about salvation. Even though she was raised in the Church and was active in our congregation, unconsciously she had the idea that she was saved . . . but just partially. When she realized that her salvation was complete in Jesus, she was overcome with a joy that had her jumping for joy.

It is my guess there are many people in the church today who think they are only partially saved. One lady long ago explained salvation to me this way: "You either is or you ain't. Sort of like being pregnant."

Do you know what is even better? Jesus is alive and interceding for we who are completely saved.

WEEK 18—TUESDAY

"Whoever dwells in the shelter of the Most High will rest in the shadow of the Almighty." Psalm 91:1 NIRV

A shelter is a place that gives temporary protection from bad weather or danger. We need such a shelter living in this dangerous world. God is not a temporary protection; He is an eternal one. There is no shelter apart from Him. Life can be very hard—even for believers—but when we dwell in the shelter of the Most High, we can find rest in His shadow.

There have been those times in my life I was outdoors when an unexpected storm came upon me. My immediate response was to find some temporary shelter until the storm blew over. In my spiritual walk with Jesus, I am learning to dwell in my shelter all the time and not just go to Him when storms hit. There is an incredible security and rest that come from abiding and dwelling in the Most High.

Need some protection? You know where to go!

Life can be harsh. Let God be your shelter.

WEEK 18–WEDNESDAY

"For where there is a testament, there must also of necessity be the death of the testator. For a testament is in force after men are dead, since it has no power at all while the testator lives."
Hebrews 9:16–17 NKJV

I've been raised on the NIV version of the Bible, so when I read the preceding verses recently, I had to ask myself, "What is a testator?" The dictionary definition is: "a person who has made a will or given a legacy." Jesus Christ is our testator. He included us in His will, but in order for us to receive our inheritance, He had to die.

We have been promised an eternal inheritance through our faith in our testator, Jesus Christ. Our inheritance will never fade away. We get to enjoy it forever. The earthly inheritances we receive from our earthly parents or relatives can be a blessing, but we can't take it with us to heaven. As recipients of Jesus's will, we get to enjoy it forever and ever. If you are a believer in Jesus Christ, you are rich!

I thank my tesator for including me in His will.

WEEK 18–THURSDAY

"If my people, who are called by my name, will humble themselves and pray and seek my face and turn from their wicked ways, then I will hear from heaven, and will forgive their sin and will heal their land." 2 Chronicles 7:14 NIV84

National Day of Prayer is observed on the first Thursday of May. Our country needs people who will commit themselves to pray for our nation on an ongoing basis. Our nation is in need of healing, but it's not a time to point a finger at all the immoral agendas that contradict our Christian beliefs. It's a time for us to look inward and follow the advice of 2 Chronicles 7:14. Take another look at this powerful verse.

God addresses those who already believe in Him ("my people, who are called by my name"). He wants us to humble ourselves, to seek His face, and turn from our wicked ways. When we do so, our God promises to hear our prayers and heal our land.

Seek the Lord today. You might not change the course of the nation, but you can change the course of another individual. You can make a difference.

Revival begins with me.

WEEK 18—FRIDAY

> *"As soon as the priests who carry the ark of the Lord—the Lord of the earth—set foot in the Jordan, its waters flowing downstream will be cut off and stand up in a heap." Joshua 3:13 NIV84*

The people of God finally were ready to enter the Promised Land, but they faced a huge obstacle—the Jordan River at flood stage. Good news: God always has a plan. He ordered the priests to carry the Ark of the Covenant up to the edge of the river and then step into the waters of the Jordan. It wasn't until they stepped out in faith that their God made a way. By literally stepping out in faith, God made the river stop and dried it up so they could pass.

Sometimes, my friends, we wait by the river's edge for God to make a way, but maybe He is waiting on us. There are times we just have to step out in faith and trust God to make a way. Scary? Yes. But imagine the "rush" when the river pauses and allows you to pass.

Maybe God is waiting for you to put your faith into action.

Catching the Moments

What moments stand out to you from this past week?

What verse of Scripture was important to you during the past week?

In seven words or fewer, describe this past week.

_____

_____

_____

_____

_____

_____

_____

_____

_____

_____

_____

_____

_____

WEEK 19—SUNDAY

"Do not forsake your mother's teaching." Proverbs 1:8 NIV 84

Don't forget Mother's Day. There are so many lessons that godly mothers can pass along to their children. Let me mention five examples from Scripture.

Sarah was the mother of Isaac (Gen. 21:6). Isaac means "he laughs," so Sarah was someone who gave birth to laughter. Thank God for moms who do that.

Hannah was the mother of Samuel (I Sam. 1:28). Thank God for mothers who know how to give their children back to God.

Elizabeth was the mother of John the Baptist (Luke 1:6). Thank God for mothers who are faithful and obedient like Elizabeth.

Mary was the mother of Jesus (Luke 1:38,48). Thank God for mothers who see themselves as humble servants.

Eunice was the mother of Timothy (2 Tim. 1:5). Thank God for mothers (and grandmothers) who are good role models.

Thank your mother and any other ones today for their incredible hearts.

Henry Ward Beecher once said, "The mother's heart is the child's schoolroom."

WEEK 19—MONDAY

"The Lord your God is with you, he is mighty to save. He will take great delight in you, he will quiet you with his love, he will rejoice over you with singing." Zephaniah 3:17 NIV 84

When you take a close look at this verse, it sounds almost too good to be true. Most of us would agree with the first sentence: Yes, I know God is with me and He is mighty to save. Hallelujah for that! I need saving.

Read on, my friend! The Lord our God takes great delight in you and rejoices over you with singing. All I can say is *wow*. For the longest time it was hard for me to imagine that God loves me that much. Why would He want to celebrate and sing over me? I heard someone say years ago, "Get over yourself and allow God to love you."

Love is not just something God does for us sinners because He feels sorry for us. Love is who He is. Can you imagine what heaven is going to be like?

My God takes delight in me.

WEEK 19–TUESDAY

> *"I praise you, Father, Lord of heaven and earth, because you have hidden these things from the wise and learned, and revealed them to little children." Matthew 11:25 NIV84*

Jesus intended the Gospel to be simple enough for even a child to understand. He had a way of speaking such profound truths in simple ways, but in our attempt to appear wise, we sometimes try to speak these simple truths in profound ways. We will never be able to understand all the wisdom of God, yet the Gospel is easy enough for a child to comprehend it. Imagine, the secrets of the kingdom of God are revealed to those with childlike hearts. Start reading the Word with childlike faith.

That doesn't mean we should stop learning and studying. God wants our relationship with Him to be one that is maturing. Paul told the Corinthians that they should "stop thinking like children. In regards to evil be infants, but in your thinking be adults."(I Cor. 14:20). What Jesus wants is a child's heart in a grown-up's head.

We are called to be childlike, not childish.

WEEK 19—WEDNESDAY

> *"There are six things the Lord hates, seven that are detestable to him." Proverbs 6:16 NIV84*

While Christ carried our sins on the cross and, by His grace, offers us forgiveness, *don't ever take sin lightly*. In verses 17–19 seven sins are listed that God hates and He finds detestable.

1. Haughty eyes or arrogance. 2. A lying tongue. 3. Hands that murder the innocent. 4. A heart that devises wicked schemes. 5. Feet that are quick to rush into evil. 6. A false witness who lies. 7. A person who stirs up conflict in the community.

There are other sins that God hates, but let's deal with what is listed for now. Guard your heart and keep yourself in Christ, your Savior. All of us are capable of committing any of these sins if we step outside of His gracious fellowship. Remember that common phrase: "God hates sin but loves the sinner."

We are all sinners who have fallen short of His glory, so what is the answer? Hate what God hates, love what God loves, and you will enjoy what God enjoys.

All of the preceding sins deal with how we relate to other people.

WEEK 19—THURSDAY

> *"As he said this, he was taken up before their very eyes, and a cloud hid him from their sight." Acts 1:9 NIV84*

Following His resurrection Jesus appeared to many of His disciples on several occasions. On the fortieth day of resurrection, He ascended before their very eyes through the clouds, back into heaven, where He sits at the right hand of His Father. There He will remain until that glorious day when He comes back through the clouds to take us home to heaven.

What an incredible experience His ascension had to be for His followers. Just image Him being lifted up from the earth while they stared in amazement. I loved what the angels told the disciples on Ascension Day: "Why do you stand here looking into the sky?" Ten days later, the Holy Spirit would fall on Pentecost, and the Church would be born.

Friends, it was to our advantage that Jesus left this world so the Holy Spirit could come into power. Let's take our heads out of the clouds. He is coming back, and we need to get to work.

Happy Ascension Day!

WEEK 19—FRIDAY

"You are our pride and joy!" I Thessalonians 2:20 MSG

I once visited a congregation where a sweet longtime member showed me their newly renovated stained-glass windows. As we walked into their sanctuary, she pointed to the windows and said, "That is the pride and joy of our church." Now, I must admit that these windows were very colorful and conveyed the Gospel message in a beautiful way, but I don't think they were intended to be the pride and joy of the Church—especially since her congregation was dying.

Paul told the Thessalonian Church that he would be so proud of them when Jesus Christ returned. They were his pride and joy. He was excited to see how the Holy Spirit had changed these individuals into powerful disciples of Jesus Christ. I must admit that the greatest joy in ministry is watching how people mature and grow in Christ. Now, that brings me joy. Changed lives still remain the best advertisement for the Church.

I don't know if there will be stained-glass windows in heaven, but I'm sure they won't be our pride and joy.

Catching the Moments

What moments stand out to you from this past week?

What verse of Scripture was important to you during the past week?

In seven words or fewer, describe this past week.

WEEK 20—SUNDAY

"Do not be misled: 'Bad company corrupts good character.'"I Corinthians 15:33 NIV84

We have to be careful whom we are hanging out with. I know Jesus has called us to go into all the world and be witnesses for Him, but it's important to ask yourself: "Who is influencing who?" Are you sowing good seed into their lives or are they sowing their bad seed into yours? Take heed to Paul's advice to the Corinthian Church: "Bad company corrupts good character."

There is a big difference between going to the lost and hanging out with bad company. Too many Christians have been pulled back into a lifestyle they have already been delivered from. It takes time to build up good character, but it doesn't take long to lose it when you hang with the wrong crowd.

There are people and lifestyles that we just have to walk away from. If we don't, our good character will be corrupted.

Jesus spent a lot of time with some bad characters, but He was secure in who He was and assured of His objective.

WEEK 20—MONDAY

"And now, friends, we ask you to honor those leaders who work so hard for you, who have been given the responsibility of urging and guiding you along in your obedience. Overwhelm them with appreciation and love!" I Thessalonians 5:12 MSG

Ministry is hard work. Even though I was blessed to serve at the same congregation for thirty-two years, there was more than one occasion when the spiritual burden of being a pastor was overwhelming. But do you know what kept me going? I was overwhelmed by the appreciation and love of incredible members. It didn't take a Pastor Appreciation

Month to experience genuine appreciation and love. I was blessed with it year-round. Not every leader was as fortunate as I was.

A good pastor or leader accepts the burden that accompanies ministry out of love for the Lord and others. Nonetheless, that burden can sometimes be heavy, and we "pastors" can be sometimes needier than the sheep we choose to shepherd.

Overwhelm your pastor with appreciation and love. Do something incredible for him or her. It just may encourage him or her to do a better job.

WEEK 20—TUESDAY

> *"Even though I walk through the valley of the shadow of death, I will fear no evil, for you are with me." Psalm 23:4 NIV84*

Dr. Donald Barnhouse was a great man of God during the beginning of the twentieth century. This story was shared following the death of his wife to cancer.

As they were driving to her funeral, Dr. Barnhouse and his three young children were still deeply grieving the death of his wife and their mother. In the midst of their tears, a large moving truck passed them on the highway and cast its shadow over their whole car. Dr. Barnhouse quickly asked his oldest daughter, "What would you rather be run over by, that truck or the shadow of the truck?" She quickly responded, "The shadow, of course." With her response, he told his children, "There is nothing to fear. Mother has only been run over by the shadow of death."

Do not fear, followers of Jesus Christ. He was run over by death so that we only have to be run over by its shadow.

WEEK 20—WEDNESDAY

"Weeping may remain for a night, but rejoicing comes in the morning." Psalm 30:5 NIV84

People are going to disappoint you. Accept it. Whether it be family, colleagues, or friends, we are going to have moments when others let us down or just plain forget us. Such moments may wound us, but they don't have to shape us. What we need to do is learn how to respond in those moments.

What usually happens when others disappoint us is that our feelings are hurt, we shed our tears, we may even have some anger or want to retaliate. Don't allow those seeds to take root in your heart. After you have had your time of tears, be quick to forgive, shake it off, and move on. Your joy will return.

Our Savior understands what it is like to have people disappoint Him. We do it all the time. I've done it to Him often, but He is so forgiving and allows me to stay in my "pity party" for only so long.

Lord, teach me how to respond to disappointment the way You do.

WEEK 20—THURSDAY

"Speak, Lord, for your servant is listening." I Samuel 3:9 NIV84

Isn't it interesting that God spoke to a child because the priest was not listening? God has not changed. He still longs to speak to His children, but the problem in most cases is that we are not listening. We are losing the ability to listen. In fact, some would even consider us odd if we said that God spoke to us. One of the most common hindrances to children hearing God's voice is unbelieving adults.

Listen to what Jesus said in John 10:27: "My sheep listen to my voice; I know them and they follow me." Has your adulthood robbed you of the childlike ability to listen to God? Our Good Shepherd still speaks to His sheep. He speaks through His Word, but He also communicates with us through the thoughts and ideas He plants in our receptive minds.

In your prayer life, allow yourself some quiet time to just listen. Prayer is communication between us and God. I don't know about you, but I'm good at speaking to God but not as good at listening to Him.

Lord, teach me how to listen.

WEEK 20—FRIDAY

> *"Some people are like seed along the path, where the word is sown. As soon as they hear it, Satan comes and takes away the word that was sown in them." Mark 4:15 NIV84*

Satan knows the power the Word of God can produce in a believer's heart. That is why one of his objectives is to do all he can to steal the Word sown into our hearts. We need to become more aware of his tactics. For example, every Sunday many people sit in various churches and listen to the Word of God. They are encouraged and filled with hope listening to the promises of our God.

Satan is fully aware of those seeds that were sown and waits for you outside of Church to take away the Word that was placed in your heart by the Holy Spirit. (Sometimes he doesn't even wait for you to leave church.) He'll cause things to happen or place people in your path that will distract you from the truth you've just received.

Prepare your hearts when you leave Church. Don't let Satan rip you off.

Catching the Moments

What moments stand out to you from this past week?

What verse of Scripture was important to you during the past week?

In seven words or fewer, describe this past week.

_____

_____

_____

_____

_____

_____

_____

_____

_____

_____

_____

_____

_____

_____

WEEK 21–SUNDAY

"Be filled with the Spirit." Ephesians 5:18 NIV84

Pentecost is the day when we celebrate the birthday of the Church. Three thousand souls were saved in one day when the Holy Spirit fell on that group of 120 people. God wants to empower His Church today so that souls will continue to be won for Jesus Christ.

We are told to "be filled with the Spirit." The literal meaning of this verse means that you are to be overcome by a power greater than your own. God does not want to control your life against your will. He wants us to humble ourselves and give Him permission to allow His Holy Spirit to make us bold witnesses for Jesus Christ.

How are we to be filled with the Holy Spirit? Don't overthink it. Very simply: Repent and believe in Jesus Christ as your personal Lord and Savior. Ask God to fill you with His Spirit. Don't be afraid of Him. Expect and believe the power of God to come. Ask God to fill you every day.

Committees, training, and gifts are not wrong, but they can't take the place of Holy Spirit power.

WEEK 21–MONDAY

"When they had all had enough to eat, he said to his disciples, 'Gather the pieces that are left over. Let nothing be wasted.'" John 6:12 NIV84

Jesus had just fed thousands of people with five small barley loaves and two small fish. What an incredible miracle! After everyone had enough to eat, He instructed His disciples to gather all the leftovers, and told them, "Let nothing be wasted." So they filled twelve baskets with the pieces of the five barley loaves from the thousands of people. Jesus did not like His miracles to be wasted.

Have you ever noticed that Jesus often had expectations of those who received His miracles? For those who were recipients of a large catch of fish, someone obviously had to clean them. For the lame beggar who was healed, he had to find a new means of income. For those who dined on bread and fish, someone had to pick up the leftovers.

Maybe the reason we don't see more miracles is because we may waste the ones we've been given.

Let nothing be wasted.

> *"But the time will come when the Anarchist will no longer be held back, but will be let loose. But don't worry. The Master Jesus will be right on his heels and blow him away. The Master appears and—puff!—the Anarchist is out of there."*
> *2 Thessalonians 2:7–8 MSG*

The Antichrist (or the Anarchist according to Eugene Peterson) is a real personal opponent of Jesus who will appear right before the end of the world. He will stand opposed to Christ and His Church with a display of counterfeit power that will deceive many. Many people have their opinions of who this man might be, but their overinterpretation goes beyond what we know in Scripture.

Don't worry, followers of Jesus. When he does appear, Jesus is only going to let him hang around for so long. And when our Savior shows up—puff—the Antichrist is outta here.

In the meantime, stay committed to God's Word. Those who stand on the Word will not be deceived by any of the lies of Satan because they are filled with truth.

Our Master Jesus has our future firmly in His hands.

WEEK 21—WEDNESDAY

"Apart from me you can do nothing." John 15:5 NIV84

Ministry is not what we do for God but what God does through us. We can do nothing apart from Him. Even Jesus expressed His dependence upon His Heavenly Father for everything He did and said. I gladly proclaim that I have an unashamed dependence upon Jesus Christ. I can do nothing unless I am attached to my vine. In fact, I am not even able to believe in Jesus in my own strength.

In *Luther's Small Catechism* he writes the following: "I believe that I cannot by my own reason or strength believe in Jesus Christ, my Lord, or come to Him; but the Holy Spirit has called me by the Gospel, enlightened me with His gifts, sanctified and kept me in the true faith."

He has empowered us to believe, so let's believe wholeheartedly. The Holy Spirit has called us, so let's respond with boldness. He has given us gifts to be used in the kingdom of God, so let's use them.

Apart from Him we can do nothing, but with Him, we can do all things.

WEEK 21—THURSDAY

"I can do all things [which He has called me to do] through Him who strengthens and empowers me [to fulfill His purpose—I am self-sufficient in Christ's sufficiency; I am ready for anything and equal to anything through Him who infuses me with inner strength and confident peace]." Philippians 4:13 AMP

I can do all things through Christ, who infuses His strength in me. When we allow a tea bag to sit in a cup of hot water, the flavor found within the tea bag will naturally be extracted into that water. The water has to do nothing but allow the tea bag to remain in the cup, and infusion will occur.

When I allow Christ to dwell in my heart through faith, His strength will naturally be infused into my life. There is no effort required on my behalf. Just let God be God and I'm ready for anything He has called me to do.

Why don't you go make yourself a cup of tea and thank God for the process of infusion—in the cup of water and in your heart?

Lord, I need Your inner strength and confident peace.

WEEK 21—FRIDAY

"When you help someone out, don't think about how it looks. Just do it—quietly and unobtrusively. That is the way your God, who conceived you in love, working behind the scenes, helps you out." Matthew 6:3–4 MSG

I just got a note in the mail from a former member—ninety years young. What a blessing this lady is. In her note she wrote: "Thank you for guiding me to Jesus in your most unobtrusive way." The first thing I did was to look up the meaning of "unobtrusive" since her vocabulary is far more advanced than mine.

I felt tremendously honored as I thought about her words. God had used me to guide her to Jesus without attracting attention to myself. (Now I'm drawing attention to myself as I share her compliment with you.)

I love those people in the Body of Christ who help others in such quiet ways. While others may not see what you are doing, that's OK. Your Heavenly Father does, and He rewards such quiet and unobtrusive service.

Think of someone who has helped you quietly and unobtrusively.

Catching the Moments

What moments stand out to you from this past week?

What verse of Scripture was important to you during the past week?

In seven words or fewer, describe this past week.

_____

_____

_____

_____

_____

_____

_____

_____

_____

_____

_____

_____

_____

_____

"Don't allow yourself to be overpowered with evil. Take the offensive—overpower evil by good!" Romans 12:21 PHILLIPS

It is not pleasant when we are attacked by evil, but it happens. It is something that all Christians should expect, because as followers of Jesus we are a threat to the kingdom of darkness. The natural reaction is an eye for an eye, a threat for a threat, and evil for evil, but we are instructed to respond supernaturally.

When evil comes, don't let it overpower you. Take the offensive! Your enemy is expecting a retaliation of evil, but we need to catch them off guard with *good*. Don't just sit back and do nothing, *be offensive!* "The weapons we fight with are not the weapons of the world. On the contrary, they have divine power to demolish strongholds." (2 Cor. 10:4).

Forgiveness, self-control, patience, and kindness are powerful weapons in the hands of spirit-filled people. They can change the hardest of hearts into repentant and obedient ones.

You have been given a power that is greater than evil. Be offensive!

"You therefore must endure hardship as a good soldier of Jesus Christ." 2 Timothy 2:3 NKJV

I never met my Uncle Vernon, but he was a good soldier in World War 2. After being wounded in 1944, he rejoined the 101st Airborne Division. He died on January 7, 1945, defending the town of Bastogne during the Battle of the Bulge. I have the letter his commanding officer sent to my grandfather, describing him as a very good soldier. He was loved and trusted by all the others who knew him. My Uncle Vernon endured some very difficult conditions just so others could be free.

As we remember those soldiers who have given their lives so that we could be free, help us to remember that we need to endure hardships as Christians. Being a follower of Jesus Christ can be hard, but with the help of the Holy Spirit, we are given a power to help us endure.

If you are facing some battles today, make the decision to please your Commanding Officer. That is what good soldiers do.

Memorial Day is a day on which those who died in active military service are remembered.

WEEK 22—TUESDAY

"There is a time for everything, and a season for every activity under the heavens: a time to weep and a time to laugh." Ecclesiastes 3:1,4 NIV84

When was the last time you had a good laugh? Not a chuckle, but a "belly laugh" that brings tears to your eyes. Those moments don't happen all the time, but we could all do with a few more of them in our daily lives. When we lose our ability to laugh, life becomes much harder to live.

Even though the Bible never tells us that Jesus laughed, I believe that when the time was right, He laughed. Yes, He was a Man of Sorrows and bore the sin of the entire world, but I'm sure there had to be those moments around a campfire when His disciples said some things that would make anyone laugh.

I pray that the Lord will break up your day with a touch of laughter. Don't take yourself too seriously. Take a crazy selfie on your phone and send it to someone close to you. Give them something to laugh about. Laughter is contagious. Spread it around.

Make today a time to laugh . . . if not for you, then for someone else.

WEEK 22–WEDNESDAY

"My God sent his angel, and he shut the mouths of the lions. They have not hurt me." Daniel 6:22 NIV84

Daniel was a man who was faithful and obedient to His God. His integrity got him thrown in with the lions, but God's grace shut the mouths of those lions. The lions may have made a lot of noise during the night, but they didn't hurt Daniel. I wonder what Daniel was doing in the midst of all the roaring? Praying is what got him thrown into the den, and I'm sure praying is what took him through.

When we choose not to compromise the Word of God in our lives, the result can often put us in difficult situations, but that is usually when God does His most miraculous work. Don't think that the Lord has abandoned you when you end up with the lions, He is just putting you in a position to see His glory at work.

Our prayer life tends to become more earnest and meaningful when we are locked up with some lions.

Dare to be a Daniel.

WEEK 22–THURSDAY

"I went out . . . examining the walls of Jerusalem, which had been broken down, and its gates, which had been destroyed." Nehemiah 2:13 NIV84

Before the rebuilding of the walls and gates of Jerusalem were to begin, Nehemiah went out into the community to see and experience what needed to be done. God met him and gave him the vision and encouragement to tackle this big job.

Following Superstorm Sandy, our congregation spent many weeks and months reaching out to the community of Far Rockaway, which had been devastated by this storm. God had put it on our hearts to reach out and help these people, but I often drove down to this area by myself just to examine the damage and catch God's vision. It was painful to see the broken homes and broken lives, but I was able to pass along some helpful information to our workers who would follow.

Sometimes we rush into ministry situations without taking the time to examine the damage. Whether you are examining a location or people, ask the Lord to show you what needs to be done.

Lord, show me what needs to be repaired and how to do it.

WEEK 22—FRIDAY

"I seek you with all my heart." Psalm 119:10 NIV84

When we are told to seek the Lord, it's a way of describing someone seeking His Presence or seeking the Face of God. You do not come to such an awesome place by merely giving the Lord five minutes every morning. When we are graciously allowed to be drawn closer to Him, we are changed by just catching a glimpse of His glory. People who merely "go to church" have no real desire to seriously seek the Lord, but when people hunger and thirst to know Him more, His presence rewards those who seek Him for intimacy.

There is more to Jesus than what we get on a Sunday morning. He longs for us to seek Him in ways that will change our lives. Don't be content with just "going to church." You have been called to seek the Lord. Seeking His face is not accomplished by our effort but reserved for those who respond to our inner desire to be closer to our Creator.

Lord, make me hungry and thirsty for more of You.

Catching the Moments

What moments stand out to you from this past week?

What verse of Scripture was important to you during the past week?

In seven words or fewer, describe this past week.

"When he saw the crowds, he had compassion on them, because they were harassed and helpless, like sheep without a shepherd." Matthew 9:36 NIV84

Years ago, our men's ministry would assist in leading a Monday night worship service at Belmont Race Track in Elmont, NY. That is the racetrack where the Belmont Stakes takes place. Most people do not know about the life that goes on behind the scenes. It is the home of 3,000 low-income workers, with 1,500 of them living on the grounds of Belmont.

One very influential person to all these people is the chaplain—a great man of God who ministers to this huge congregation. Most of them do not gather to worship, so he goes to them. He reaches out to this needy flock and shows them the genuine and uncompromising love of God in practical ways.

When our men's ministry attended the sparsely attended worship services on Monday nights, our job was simply to "love on" the people who came.

There is something powerful about just having compassion on people who are harassed and helpless (aren't we all?).

"Those who accepted his message were baptized." Acts 2:41 NIV84

Karen was raised in a Jewish household and was raised to think of Christians as an enemy of her religion. Through the invitation of a friend, she started coming to Church and listened attentively to Good News about Jesus. She became a believer in her Messiah, Jesus, just through listening to the Word of God. One day she came to see me and said, "I need to be baptized." She didn't ask to be baptized; she *needed* to be baptized. So in a private ceremony, because of family opposition, I baptized her in the name of the Father and of the Son and of the Holy Spirit.

Karen was brought to tears, and the Lord's Presence rushed into that sanctuary. There were only four of us in the room, but what a powerful moment that was for all of us. Years later she would write that the day she was baptized was the most important day in her life.

Sometimes we forget what God is able to do through the sacrament of baptism.

WEEK 23—TUESDAY

> *"I will still be the same when you are old and gray, and I will take care of you. I created you. I will carry you and always keep you safe." Isaiah 46:4 CEV*

As we get older, God does not change. We do, but He remains the same. Even when we get old and gray (or old and bald), He has promised to take care of us. While we need Him in every stage of our life, we become dependent upon the Lord in different ways when we enter our senior years.

As I turn seventy, I'm becoming more and more aware of the Lord's care of me. He's the same God as when I was twenty, but now I'm appreciating His presence even more. He's taken care of me all these years and will continue to do so as long as I remain on this earth.

If you are in your senior years, be assured that God has your back (and feet, heart, knees, etc.). If you haven't entered this wonderful season of your life, pray for someone who has.

No one is too young or too old to be used by God. You are always at the perfect age.

WEEK 23-WEDNESDAY

"The fear of the Lord is the beginning of wisdom." Psalm 111:10 NIV84

We have watered down the meaning of what it means to "fear the Lord." Many people in the Church say that the word "fear" does not mean "to be afraid"; it just means "to show respect." Tell that to Moses as he took off his sandals and hid his face from the Burning Bush. Tell that to Isaiah as he got a glimpse into the throne room of God and said, "Woe to me." Tell that to John when he fell over as dead before Jesus in the book of Revelation. If God appeared to us as He did to these men, we would be awestruck.

God loves us and has given us access to Him through Jesus Christ, but He should still make our knees shake when we come into His Holy Presence. It is incredible that we can have a personal relationship with our Sovereign and All-Powerful God.

It's amazing how wise we can become when we show a healthy fear of the Lord.

WEEK 23-THURSDAY

"Submit yourselves, then, to God. Resist the devil, and he will flee from you." James 4:7 NIV84

Most people are familiar with the second part of this verse: "Resist the devil and he will flee from you." If we want to see the second part of this verse come to pass in our lives, we must give attention to the first part—"Submit yourselves to God." The devil is not afraid of you, so you can resist him all you want and even curse him all you want, but he's not going to flee until you are submitted to God.

When we yield to God's authority and will in our lives, we can stand firm against the devil and he will flee or back off. He'll return again, which means we must stay submitted to our Lord. He tried to bring down Jesus in the wilderness, but Jesus spoke the Word with authority (because He was submitted to His Father). Submission does not make you weak; it makes you strong.

Are there some areas of your life that are not submitted to God?

WEEK 23—FRIDAY

"Sirs, what must I do to be saved?" Acts 16:30 NIV84

Just because someone sits in church week after week doesn't mean that they are saved. You do not become a car by sitting in a garage and you do not become a hamburger by sitting in McDonald's. Neither do you become a Christian by merely sitting in a pew. You become a Christian by believing and confessing Jesus Christ as your personal Lord and Savior.

When asking people if they would go to heaven when they died, I've had some people say, "Well, I think so. I was baptized. I was confirmed." But they didn't talk about Jesus. I've even had a couple of people refuse to answer because they said their faith was personal and they never talk to anyone about it. While our salvation is not based upon our merit, it does require that we acknowledge Jesus Christ before others (Matt. 10:32–33).

If you are not sure of your salvation, put your pride aside and pray with someone at church.

Your assurance of salvation is only a prayer away.

Catching the Moments

What moments stand out to you from this past week?

What verse of Scripture was important to you during the past week?

In seven words or fewer, describe this past week.

_____

_____

_____

_____

_____

_____

_____

_____

_____

_____

_____

_____

> *"Let us not become weary in doing good, for at the proper time we will reap a harvest if we do not give up."* **Galatians 6:9 NIV84**

On the last night of my mission trip to India, I had the humbling experience of speaking to about thirty people who were in training to be church planters in New Delhi. These incredible disciples had already planted many churches and had been persecuted in the process. As I spoke through an interpreter, I used Galatians 6:9 as the text for my sermon. The hungry students hung on every word of scripture, and when I was finished, I taught them a simple chorus: "Don't give up, Someone really loves you. Don't give up, Someone really cares. Don't give up, Someone really loves you, and that Someone is the Lord."

As we sang this short chorus, people began to weep. On their own they began to commit themselves to not becoming weary to doing good. I was so humbled that I began to weep.

Don't give up, my friends. Don't become weary in doing good for the Lord.

The harvest is coming.

> *"Above all, love each other deeply, because love covers a multitude of sins." I Peter 4:8 NIV84*

God's love covers a multitude (that means a lot) of sins. There is not a sin that our God won't forgive. Your greatest sin is never bigger than the grace of our God. Nothing can separate us from the love of God that is found in Christ Jesus, our Lord. That is Good News!

But here is a point to put in perspective: God's love can't cover over the sins that we cover up. It is kind of ridiculous to think that we can hide anything from God, but we still do. Pride, shame, and ignorance can sometimes prevent laying all our sins on the Lord. Jesus died so that we could be forgiven, so why do we cover up some of our sins, rather than confessing them to Him?

When we cover up our sins, we not only hinder a strong relationship with Jesus; we also hinder our relationship with other people. Don't cover up what God wants to cover over.

Whenever you cover the sins of your neighbor, love runs deep.

WEEK 24—TUESDAY

> *"This is what the Lord Almighty says: 'These people say, "The time has not yet come to rebuild the Lord's house."'"*
> *Haggai 1:2 NIRV*

After the Jews had left Babylonian captivity, they returned to their home and set out to rebuild the temple. The first thing they did was to lay its foundation, which is the most important part of any building. But then they went about their own business for sixteen years. The people had become so self-absorbed with their own homes that they had no time to build God's house. That's when the Lord sent the prophet Haggai to the scene.

This story reminds me a lot of the Church. People can enter a new life of freedom by laying the foundation of faith in Jesus Christ. But all too often, after laying the foundation, people go about their own business and neglect building the kingdom of God.

After Haggai brought the Word of the Lord and helped the people to refocus, they resumed the building of the temple. After sixteen years of inactivity, they finished building the temple in four years.

Great things can happen when people come together.

WEEK 24–WEDNESDAY

"Don't let anyone look down on you because you are young, but set an example for the believers in speech, in conduct, in love, in faith and in purity." I Timothy 4:12 NIV84

Jason was a young man who was a believer in Jesus Christ and on a path to an exciting future when he died in a car accident at only eighteen years old. In the last couple years of his life, he had found his identity in Christ and began to write out a number of personal prayers. With his mother's permission, I share just a few lines from a letter he wrote to God shortly before he died:

"Thank You for my pastor, Steve Roth. Thank You for his wife, Alison. Lord, they and others have been a help through You. . . . Forgive me of my sins, Jesus. . . . Lord, let me not fear anybody but You. Let me be ready for Your coming, Lord, but meanwhile let me live right and take life seriously. . . . Give me a Spirit of boldness, Lord."

Well done, Jason. Great is your reward in heaven.

WEEK 24–THURSDAY

"A wise person is hungry for truth, while the fool feeds on trash." Proverbs 15:14 NLT

What an interesting contrast: hungry for truth vs. feeding on trash. Everyone claims to be seeking the truth, but the wise not only seek it; they are hungry for it. People who are truly hungry for truth will search it out in times of worship and prayer, and will strive after it until it is found.

Fools don't accept the truth, even when it knocks on their door. "Feeding on trash" sounds disgusting, because it is disgusting. I know from experience, because I've fed on some of it in my life. I think we all have.

Truth satisfies and brings contentment. The wise person finds truth in the person of Jesus Christ, because He told us that He was the truth (John 14:6). Once you have tasted truth, your spiritual tastebuds change. Psalm 34:8 tells us to "taste and see that the Lord is good."

Ask the Lord the change your spiritual appetite, and search His Word daily for truth.

Is there any trash you need to remove from your diet?

WEEK 24–FRIDAY

> *"Grow in the grace and knowledge of our Lord and Savior Jesus Christ." 2 Peter 3:18 NIV84*

Many people associate the summer months with vacation time. It's a time away from school or maybe a time away from the job or just a time of R&R. Most of us love summertime. To the farmer, summer is a time of growth. He wants to see progress in all the sowing that took place in his fields.

As we begin another summer, and as you enjoy your vacations and R&R, ask the Lord to give you a SONG—or to put it another way: "Lord, give me a **S**ummer **O**f **N**ew **G**rowth." What can you do over the summer months to develop spiritually? Set some goals that will help you grow in your relationship with Jesus and other people. Think of the harvest that you could possibly reap!

Make the following confession to the Lord: "Lord, I don't want to stay the same. I want to grow. Show me how to make progress in my walk with You."

Give me a SONG.

Catching the Moments

What moments stand out to you from this past week?

What verse of Scripture was important to you during the past week?

In seven words or fewer, describe this past week.

"So he got up and went to his father. But while he was still a long way off, his father saw him and was filled with compassion for him." Luke 15:20 NIV84

During my college years, ages eighteen to twenty-two, I went off the grid. What I mean is that I chose to party far more than I did to study. I moved from one college to another as I moved further away from the values I was raised with. EventuallyI was thrown out because of my grades and had to come home to parents who had sacrificed to pay for my prodigal life. As I arrived home, I was ashamed and ready for any consequences that I had earned.

As I walked in the front door of my parents' home, something incredible happened. My father met me at the door and welcomed me home with open arms. I deserved nothing, but I was offered grace.

I had grown up in a home where I understood the meaning of grace. Knowledge of grace helped shape my life, but the experience of grace helped change my life.

Happy Father's Day. May God's grace abound in your relationships.

"So Moses was trained in all the wisdom of the Egyptians and was powerful in his words and deeds." Acts 7:22 NET

Here is an interesting concept to ponder: God trained Moses in a palace to use him in a desert, and He trained Joseph in a desert to use him in a palace. While our spiritual training can differ, and while God's uses can also differ, our purpose and message remain the same. God wants to be glorified and wants everyone to believe in His Son, Jesus Christ.

God trained me for the pastoral ministry by cleaning houses and offices for five years. I didn't go to the seminary but spent my time serving others by cleaning their toilets. It was a humbling education, but it truly helped me to have the heart of a pastor. My ordination was not accepted by a few of my colleagues, but that's OK. What I lacked in education, I gained in understanding my role as a servant.

God trains us all differently, but our message remains the same: believe in Jesus Christ and you shall be saved.

WEEK 25–TUESDAY

"When I fed them, they were satisfied; when they were satisfied, they became proud; then they forgot me." Hosea 13:6 NIV84

The nature of man is no different today than it was thousands of years ago. There is a pattern that we seem to follow from one generation to the next: man is in need, God graciously responds, man is blessed, man becomes satisfied, man becomes proud, man forgets God. I know that is a very simple evaluation, but that is a pattern that the human race has followed from the Book of Genesis until now.

When our gracious God feeds us and provides for us, we need to be on guard. Don't let satisfaction turn into pride and then into forgetfulness. Thank the Lord daily for what we have been given. Worship the Giver, not just the gifts He gives.

Even though we are a fickle people, God remains the same. He says in Hosea 14:4, "I will heal their waywardness and love them freely, for my anger has turned away from them."

When you are well cared for, don't forget the God who did it.

> *"Simon, Simon, Satan has asked to sift you like wheat. But I have prayed for you, Simon, that your faith may not fail. And when you have turned back, strengthen your brothers." Luke 22:31–32 NIV84*

"Resilient: able to withstand or recover quickly from difficult conditions." I have a deep admiration for resilient people. All of us have moments when we get knocked down or beaten up, but there is a tremendous witness when people are quick to bounce back and then encourage others to do the same. The Apostle Peter was such a man.

We will all go through periods of testing and trial, but isn't it wonderful to know that Jesus is praying for you? Peter was able to bounce back and recover from his testing because he knew that His Savior had not given up on him.

Jesus has not given up on you either. He supplies you with His power to recover; and when you have recovered, make sure you help others to do the same.

Ask the Lord: "Today, with Your help, let me to become more resilient."

WEEK 25—THURSDAY

> *"Surrender your heart to God, turn to him in prayer." Job 11:13 CEV*

I once got a recall letter from the Hyundai Dealer where I purchased my car. They were requesting that I return my car so they could make some necessary repairs and adjustments to prevent future problems. These adjustments would not cost me anything except my willingness to surrender my car to their care for an undetermined period of time.

God sends me "recall" letters all the time. I find myself in need of repair from time to time (and I'm not just talking about physical issues). My spirit is in need of adjustment and only God can fix it. I know that! I want that! I need that! Who doesn't?

Even though it usually costs us nothing, why do we sometimes hesitate to have God make the necessary adjustments or repairs in our life? Surrender! God does his best work when we willingly surrender ourselves to His care, but that means giving up control. Ugh! That's hard for control freaks.

Lord, thank You for sending me all those recall letters I read every morning in Scripture.

WEEK 25—FRIDAY

"The important thing is that in every way, whether from false motives or true, Christ is preached. And because of this I rejoice." Philippians 1:18 NIV84

While on summer vacation many years ago, I was sitting on the porch trying to come to grips with the meaning of this verse. Was Paul saying that motives are not important? I asked the Lord, "What does this mean?"

As I looked out on the lake, I saw my son canoeing with some of his friends. Almost immediately I had this thought rush into my mind: *If your son was drowning and needed to be saved, would the motives of his rescuers really matter to you? No! I wouldn't care what someone's motives were, as long as his life was saved.*

Obviously, motives are important to the Lord, but when it comes to salvation of one's soul, there is power in the Word being preached—even if the preacher's motives are false.

God will deal with the motives, but let the Word be preached—whether the motives are false or true.

Catching the Moments

What moments stand out to you from this past week?

What verse of Scripture was important to you during the past week?

In seven words or fewer, describe this past week.

_____

_____

_____

_____

_____

_____

_____

_____

_____

_____

> *"And Elisha prayed, 'Open his eyes, Lord, so that he may see.'"*
> *2 Kings 6:17 NIRV*

The king of Aram was hunting down the prophet Elisha. When the king found his location, he sent his army to surround the place where he was staying. Elisha's servant got up early and went outside to see an army of horses and chariots circling the hill around them. He was frightened and rushed in to tell the prophet. Elisha wasn't concerned and told his servant, "Don't be afraid. Those who are with us are more than those who are with them." Then he prayed, "Lord, open his eyes so that he can see." The servant went outside once again. The enemy's army was still there, but now he saw an army of angels around them.

When we are attacked by enemy forces, we must learn to walk by faith and not by what we see. We must always remember that *those who are with us are more than who are with them.*

It is always good to pause and ask the Lord, "Open my eyes so that I can see."

> *"I well remember them, and my soul is downcast within me. Yet this I call to mind and therefore I have hope: Because of the LORD's great love we are not consumed, for his compassions never fail. They are new every morning; great is your faithfulness." Lamentations 3:20–23 NIV84*

Pete served the city of New York as a fireman for the FDNY. He spent many days at Ground Zero following the tragic event of 9/11. Besides the trauma of search and rescue, there were the dozens of funerals and memorial services to attend over the next several weeks. A therapist eventually told Pete that he had to stop attending these services. He eventually retired from the FDNY, broken, downcast, and an alcoholic.

Over time he stopped drinking and started coming to church again. Jesus changed him from a broken man into a man of God. He would eventually become an elder in our congregation and a close friend of mine. While the memories of 9/11 are still with him, Jesus has given him hope to move forward.

The traumatic events of the past can hurt us, but they don't have to consume us.

WEEK 26—TUESDAY

> *"He has shown you, O mortal, what is good. And what does the Lord require of you? To act justly and to love mercy and to walk humbly with your God." Micah 6:8 NIRV*

God doesn't require a lot from us—just those things that would enhance our relationship with Him: act justly, love mercy, and walk humbly with your God. We are not saved by obeying these words, but we can't obey them unless we are saved.

"Act justly" means to show justice. The desire to receive justice is not enough; we must be just in the way we treat others. "Love mercy" means that we love giving away mercy as much as we do receiving it. "Walk humbly with your God" means you are willing to take a back seat to Jesus. Just being with Him is not enough; we must be willing to walk with Him too.

It is not enough to talk the talk; we've got to be willing to walk the walk.

Act right, love right, walk right. That's all God requires.

WEEK 26—WEDNESDAY

"You should not be surprised at my saying, 'You must be born again.'" John 3:7 NIV84

Do not apologize to anyone for what this verse is communicating. Jesus is clearly saying that if we want to see the kingdom of God, we *must* be born again. Those are Jesus's words, not mine. Let me say it a different way: the only way for us to become Christians is if we are born again.

We are not saved merely by being baptized as a baby or being confirmed within the Church or being a member of your church council or being a good person. We are saved when we are born again. So what does "born again" mean? One of the rules of interpretation is to let Scripture interpret Scripture. Read some other verses about salvation: John 3:16, Romans 10:9, Ephesians 2:8–9.

If you are not sure that you are born again, pray from your heart: "Jesus, forgive me, I'm a sinner. I believe that You died and rose again. I confess You as my Lord and my Savior. Let Your Holy Spirit give me new life and understanding of what it means to be born again."

WEEK 26—THURSDAY

"These women were helping to support them out of their own means." Luke 8:3 NIV84

There were many women who had been blessed with the means to support Jesus and His disciples in their ministry. Their lives had obviously been changed by meeting Jesus, and they were blessed to help them with food or finances to meet any of their needs.

It is important for us to support others in their ministry. It might be missionaries to a foreign country, a homeless ministry in your community, or paying for someone else to go on a short-term mission trip.

There are so many opportunities for us to support others out of our own means.

If God has blessed you with the means, why not find a way to support someone else in ministry? Your giving will help people experience the love of God in real ways. You may not be able to travel to the jungles of South America, but you can support someone who is called by God to go there.

Your giving may bring salvation to souls, who you may meet in heaven.

WEEK 26–FRIDAY

> *"Now this was the sin of your sister Sodom: She and her daughters were arrogant, overfed and unconcerned; they did not help the poor and needy. They were haughty and did detestable things before me." Ezekiel 16:49–50 NIV84*

Some people think that the reason God destroyed the city of Sodom (and Gomorrah) is because of their sexual permissiveness. According to the preceding verse, that was only one of the reasons. Sodom's sins were arrogance, overindulgence, lack of concern, neglect of the poor and needy, haughtiness, and detestable things. Before we point the finger at Sodom, it might be wise to take a close look at our own country. America is just as guilty as Sodom. So what do we do?

First, ask the Lord to forgive us personally for where we have missed the mark. Don't go pointing the finger of accusation at our country when we are guilty of being arrogant, overfed, and unconcerned. Second, pray for our country that our leaders might examine their success in light of God's Word. Third, we are the Body of Christ and have been placed here to make a difference in the lives of others.

Forgive us, Lord.

Catching the Moments

What moments stand out to you from this past week?

What verse of Scripture was important to you during the past week?

In seven words or fewer, describe this past week.

_____

_____

_____

_____

_____

_____

_____

_____

_____

_____

_____

_____

_____

WEEK 27—SUNDAY

"Live as people who are free, not using your freedom as a cover-up for evil, but living as servants of God." I Peter 2:16 ESV

I thank God for the privilege of living in America. While our country is far from perfect, we have been blessed with a freedom that many other countries long for. It would do us all well to live in some other foreign country for a while, where freedom does not exist. We might begin to see the benefits of freedom as privileges and not just rights.

I love how Peter talks about freedom in the preceding verse: live free, but don't use our freedom as a cover-up for evil. That is true as followers of Christ and also true as patriotic citizens. Our freedom was built upon the backs and reputations of those who served.

As we celebrate the independence of our country, it is good to recall the words of JFK:"Ask not what your country can do for you, ask what you can do for your country." Live free and serve well.

Happy Independence Day!

WEEK 27—MONDAY

"Who has measured the waters in the hollow of his hand . . ." Isaiah 40:12 NIV84

Take a good look at your hand. Form a cup and take a look at the hollow of your hand. How much water could that hold? Now, try to imagine that our awesome God is able to measure the oceans of this world in the hollow of His hand. On the surface there are about 322,280,000 cubic miles of water. Now multiply 322,280,000 (mile by mile by mile) according to each mile of depth. God says, "I got it all right here in the hollow of my hand." Now that is a definition of "awesome."

We have watered down the meaning of "awesome." We'll say things such as: "That new iPhone is awesome" or "That new car is awesome." No, God is awesome.

This same God who holds the waters of the world in the hollow of His hand is the One who holds us tenderly as a shepherd holds his sheep. My life is in His hands, and He knows exactly what is going on in my world.

Our God is awesome!

WEEK 27—TUESDAY

> *"And my God will meet all your needs according to his glorious riches in Christ Jesus." Philippians 4:19 NIV84*

It is easy to quote this promise to someone else in need, but what about believing it for yourself? We serve a God of abundance. He will never run out of resources. His capacity to bless each of us is unlimited. He owns the cattle on a thousand hills (Ps. 50:10), and as my wife usually says, "Lord, we only need one of your cows."

We all have needs that have to be met. Whether they are financial, physical, emotional, or spiritual, our God has promised to meet all our needs. And where are God's riches found? In Christ Jesus.

If you are in need, turn your attention to Jesus. Seek Him first, and all your other needs will be given to you (Matt. 6:33). Don't put God into a box and limit what He can provide. If He can feed thousands of people from a little bit of fish and bread, He can certainly take care of your needs.

God will provide. Trust Him!

> *"Jesus replied, 'If anyone loves me, he will obey my teaching.'"*
> *John 14:23 NIV84*

Throughout Scripture we have been called to obey our God. I once heard a pastor say that we should not overemphasize obedience. He said it's very easy to become "works righteousness"–minded. Imagine a son telling his parents that the reason he didn't obey them was because he didn't want to become legalistic. Jesus said, "If you love me, you'll obey me."

We do not obey Jesus so that He will love us more. We obey Him because He loves us already. Obviously there will be moments when we fail in our obedience to Jesus, but we overcomplicate its meaning or overthink it. Just do it.

Wayne lived in Pennsylvania but worked in NYC. He also was an elder at our church and the youth director. I once asked him, "How are you able to make that commute every day?" His response to me was, "Pastor, I just do it and don't overthink it."

When it comes to obedience to Jesus, "Just do it. Don't overthink it."

If you love Him, you'll obey Him.

WEEK 27-THURSDAY

> *"So David triumphed over the Philistine with a sling and*
> *a stone; without a sword in his hand he struck down the*
> *Philistine and killed him." I Samuel 17:50 NIV84*

We never get tired of the David and Goliath story—when the little guy defies the odds and does the unexpected. It is always good to reread that story every now and then.

We need more little guys in the Church who are willing to stand up and defy the odds. We need people who are able to speak through a curtain of doubt and say, "We can do this." We need more people who are more concerned about the honor of their God and less of their own.

I know some Davids, and I just love being around them. God uses them to help me to aim high—to pick up my stones and do what needs to be done.

Don't let your giants that you are facing have the last word. Read the story again, then go out and stand up for your God. Others may laugh, but when giants begin to fall . . . well, you know what I mean.

You and God can defy the odds.

WEEK 27—FRIDAY

> *"Be unceasing and persistent in prayer." I Thessalonians 5:17 AMP*

I have a friend who has a wonderful personal ministry of sending out a group text every weekday morning with a verse of scripture or an encouraging word. I look forward to it. Every Friday she concludes her text with these words: "Stay prayed up and have a wonderful weekend!" Thank you, Maureen, for using technology to build others up.

We need to stay prayed up. Prayer is not something that we do when our backs are against the wall. It should be a habitual part of our day. We need to be unceasing and persistent in prayer. That does not mean that we take the posture of prayer 24/7. It means that we must stay in constant communication with our God. Thank Him throughout the day. Pray for those people you meet in the store. Ask Him for that parking space. Ask Him about all the little decisions you have to make throughout the day.

Chances are you might look at the phone every minute. How about connecting with God whenever you can?

Stay prayed up and have a wonderful weekend.

WEEK 27–SATURDAY

Catching the Moments

What moments stand out to you from this past week?

What verse of Scripture was important to you during the past week?

In seven words or fewer, describe this past week.

_____

_____

_____

_____

_____

_____

_____

_____

> *"Now Jesus himself was about thirty years old when he began his ministry." Luke 3:23 NIV84*

Jesus, our Messiah, began his earthly ministry when He was thirty years old. Likewise, David was thirty when He began his reign as king of Israel, and a Levite began his service within the temple at the same age.

When I was thirty years old, God told me that He was calling me into the ministry. Alison and I had been married for four years; our daughter, Jenn, was still a baby, and we had no money. But it was in that stage of my life that the Holy Spirit began to open my eyes to the Word of God. I fell in love with Jesus and had a longing to serve Him and worship Him.

What was significant about the age of thirty in your life? Or if you haven't reached that age yet, what are your expectations? While each year of our life is important, there is something about the age of thirty that is important in our Christian journey.

Joseph was thirty years old when he entered the service of Pharaoh king of Egypt.

> *"But in your hearts set apart Christ as Lord. Always be prepared to give an answer to everyone who asks you to give the reason for the hope that you have. But do this with gentleness and respect." I Peter 3:15 NIV84*

Always be prepared to give an answer to people who ask you, "Why do you have so much hope?" That's good advice! But here's the thing to ponder: if our lives are not displaying hope, people are not going to ask us that question.

How do we become a person who has hope in the future? It starts by setting apart Christ as Lord of your life. That means we have to allow Jesus Christ to be number one in our lives. He is not just one of the important people in our life; He wants to be number one.

When we honor Him by allowing Him to be Lord of our lives, hope begins to grow in our hearts and show in how we live our lives. Hope is a refreshing characteristic that others will notice. Be prepared to tell others why.

Without Christ, there is no lasting hope.

WEEK 28—TUESDAY

"There's nothing so delicious as the taste of gossip! It melts in your mouth." Proverbs 18:8 CEV

Gossip—there's something about it that appeals to each of us. *Did you know about John's shady past? Did you hear what happened to Joe after he left work? Did you know what Mary did before she moved here? Etc. etc. etc.* There is that fine line to where sharing a prayer need can cross over into gossip.

Whenever you hear "juicy" information about someone, do you have a need to tell someone else about it right away? If we do, we should always ask ourselves what possible good will come out of passing along this information. In our attempt to justify ourselves, we can make our gossip appear very spiritual. If the Lord should allow you to hear some information about someone else, maybe He wanted you to hear it . . . and no one else.

I pray that all of us will lose our taste for gossip.

If you should hear blatant gossip taking place in the Church, maybe the Lord has allowed you to hear it so that you can put an end to it.

WEEK 28–WEDNESDAY

"Nevertheless I have this against you, that you have left your first love." Revelation 2:4 NKJV

Jesus commended the Ephesus Church for many things they were doing well. They were hard workers, had perseverance and discernment of false teachers, and even endured some hardships for the name of Christ. On the surface, everything looked good—active people and sound doctrine. But then Jesus gave them a "nevertheless." He told them that they had left their first love. They were doing all the right things, but they had left Him out of it.

Jesus wants our relationship with Him to remain fresh, new, and spontaneous. If you have left such a relationship with Him, you haven't lost it. There is still hope: repent and come back to your first love.

It is obvious that just being active in a congregation with sound doctrine is not enough. How would Jesus describe your congregation? After commending you for what you're doing well, would there be a "nevertheless"?

Our personal relationship with Jesus Christ needs to remain a priority in our Church life and our personal life.

WEEK 28–THURSDAY

"He displays His power in the whirlwind and the storm." Nahum 1:3 NLT

I've grown to respect the power of Texas thunderstorms. You never know what to expect when one of them blows through your neighborhood. It makes your knees shake when one of those thunderbolts cracks above your home and the sirens start blasting a tornado warning. Our weakness becomes so obvious when God displays His power in nature.

Whenever one of those severe storms approaches our neighborhood, I am reminded of the power of our God. The same God who displays His power in the whirlwind and the storm wants to display His power in us. And it's in our weakness that God's power is made perfect (2 Cor. 12:9).

When God's perfect power is displayed through weak vessels, all of us are filled with awe. Have you lost respect for the power of God? Have you grown used to sunny skies and gentle breezes? Every now and then it is good to experience a storm in order for God's power to be on display.

It is better to be in the storm with Jesus than anywhere else without Him.

WEEK 28—FRIDAY

"Rise in the presence of the aged, show respect for the elderly and revere your God. I am the Lord." Leviticus 19:32 NIV84

Curtis is an amazing man of God. His stories about life are fascinating and encourage us that we can do all things through Christ who strengthens us. Oh, the stories! God has orchestrated his whole life. He was a black marine during World War II and a NYC policeman during the 1950s and '60s. After retiring as a cop, he began a new career as a flight traffic controller and eventually a federal marshall for Pan Am Airways. He worked security at the Martin Luther King "I Have a Dream" speech in Washington, DC.

At the age of ninety, he and his wife started coming to our church. He became a member of Good Shepherd Church, a part of our men's ministry, and a trustee on our church council. He is a kind man who is full of wisdom and encourages those who hang around him.

Rise in the presence of people who have lived a long and prosperous life, and ask them their story.

Catching the Moments

What moments stand out to you from this past week?

What verse of Scripture was important to you during the past week?

In seven words or fewer, describe this past week.

_____

_____

_____

_____

_____

_____

_____

_____

_____

_____

_____

_____

WEEK 29—SUNDAY

"I came that they may have life, and have it abundantly." John 10:10 NASB

Jesus came into this world to bring us life. Not just where we will spend eternal life in heaven, but He came to bring us life, abundant life, *now*. He wants us to experience the joy and purpose of life in our everyday life.

I knew a man years ago who would always respond to my "How are you?" with the words "Existing! I'm just existing!" One day I pulled him aside after church and asked to talk with him. I explained to him that Jesus did not come into this world so that we could merely exist. He came so we might have life, and have it abundantly. I asked him to start asking Jesus for an abundant life and not just one where he existed. His confession and his countenance changed over the next few months.

If you ask Jesus to experience His abundant life, He may just give it to you. That's why He came.

The abundant life is not measured in dollars and cents.

WEEK 29—MONDAY

"The wind blows wherever it pleases. You hear its sound, but you cannot tell where it comes from or where it is going. So it is with everyone born of the Spirit." John 3:8 NIV84

One of the characteristics of wind is that it is unpredictable. If it wants to blow from the north, it will do so. If it wants to blow at 26 MPH, it will do so. So is the working of the Holy Spirit in the lives of those born of the Spirit. He is always dependable but not always predictable. For example, a blind man was brought to Jesus to be healed. Jesus did something very unpredictable: He spit on the man's eyes in order that he might see. Why did Jesus do that? Maybe Jesus was teaching us not to depend upon methods when we pray for others but to depend upon the Holy Spirit in us.

Don't put God into a box and limit how He can work. While the Holy Spirit will never violate the Word of God, occasionally He might blow in some unpredictable ways.

Here's a prayer for you to pray: "Holy Spirit, blow wherever you please in my life."

WEEK 29—TUESDAY

"You forgave the iniquity of your people and covered all their sins." Selah Psalm 85:2 NIV84

The word *Selah* is used seventy-four times in the Hebrew Bible—seventy-one times in Psalms and three times in Habakkuk. While there are different interpretations of this word's meaning, I like how the Amplified Bible translates it: "pause, and think of that." So in the preceding text, David is telling the reader that our God has forgiven our iniquities and covered all of our sins. *Pause a moment and think about that!*

Has the message of forgiveness become so routine that it doesn't excite us anymore? It would do us well to pause and think about what we are reading in the Bible.

Jesus Christ took all my sins and carried them on the cross. *Selah.*

I have been forgiven and cleansed by the blood of Jesus. *Selah.*

I don't have to live in guilt of my sins because of God's grace. *Selah.*

God has given me the power to forgive others the way He has forgiven me. *Selah.*

Isn't God's forgiveness incredible?

WEEK 29—WEDNESDAY

"Noah was a righteous man, blameless among the people of his time, and he walked with God." Genesis 6:9 NIV84

When mankind's wickedness on earth had become so great, God raised up Noah. What an incredible man of faith. For one hundred years, he endured the ridicule of other people as he built the ark. He was a righteous man who walked faithfully with his God in the midst of an evil generation. His righteousness did not come from his good works, but his good works came from his righteousness.

Noah was mentioned fifty times in the Bible. Why so many times? Maybe the Lord wanted us to see what it means to "walk with God." He remained faithful even when others mocked him. He remained faithful to his calling—which resulted in the salvation of his family.

How is your walk with God? When God gives you an assignment, are you faithful to complete it? Don't give up. Your faithfulness may result in the salvation of your whole family and many others in generations to come.

Walk with the King today.

WEEK 29—THURSDAY

"Bring me back from gray exile, put a fresh wind in my sails!" Psalm 51:12 MSG

The doldrums are regions of the Atlantic and Pacific Oceans around sections of the equator that have little if any wind. These areas that would be void of any winds were a very dangerous problem for ships in the past that depended solely on the winds to propel them. Ships stuck in the doldrums could be stuck for weeks at a time.

We depend upon the winds of the Holy Spirit to propel us in life, but there are times when we get stuck in our own doldrums. Have you ever been there? Your spiritual movement has come to a halt and no matter what you try, nothing works. What you need is the Holy Spirit to put some fresh wind in your sails.

If you are stuck in the doldrums, don't despair. Repent and turn to God so that times of refreshing may come (Acts 3:19).

Ask Jesus to put some fresh wind in your sails so that you may allow Him to propel you to a new place of growth.

WEEK 29–FRIDAY

> *"Praise him, sun and moon, praise him, all you shining stars."*
> *Psalm 148:3 NIV84*

There are many references in Scripture that talk about heaven and earth praising God. Praise Him—sun, moon, stars, mountains, rivers, trees, etc. You may ask, "How do these objects of God's creation praise Him?" Whenever the Lord creates anything, He does so with a purpose. And when His creation fulfills its purpose, it brings praise to their Creator. When the river flows, it brings praise to God. When a tree blossoms and bears fruit, it brings praise to God. When the sun brings light and heat to the earth, it brings praise to God.

You have been created with a purpose, and when we fulfill our purpose for what we were created, we bring praise to our Creator. It's not just through the singing of hymns that we praise the Lord; it's also in fulfilling our purpose.

Don't let the sun, moon, and stars "outpraise" you today. Don't overcomplicate your life. Give, serve, love, pray, laugh, sing! Fulfill your purpose!

You find your purpose by seeking your Creator.

Catching the Moments

What moments stand out to you from this past week?

What verse of Scripture was important to you during the past week?

In seven words or fewer, describe this past week.

_____

_____

_____

_____

_____

_____

_____

_____

_____

_____

_____

_____

_____

WEEK 30—SUNDAY

"So that Christ may dwell in your hearts through faith."
Ephesians 3:17 NIV84

The Apostle Paul was speaking to people who were already believers in Jesus Christ. So I once asked myself, "Doesn't He already dwell in their hearts through faith?" As I studied this passage, I looked for what Paul was trying to impress upon them. While He continues to dwell in our hearts through faith, one of the commentators put it this way: "So that Christ might finally settle down and feel completely at home in your hearts through your faith."

There are many people who have never let Christ settle down and feel completely at home in their lives because they feel unworthy. Let me tell you a secret: You are unworthy. We all are! But Christ's love for us is not based upon our worthiness or our performance. That's why they call it *grace.*

He lives in us through the power of His Holy Spirit and wants to settle down and feel at home in our lives. Will you let Him?

Make Yourself at home, Jesus.

WEEK 30—MONDAY

"He broke into pieces the bronze snake Moses had made, for
up to that time the Israelites had been burning incense to it."
2 Kings 18:4 NIV84

The Lord had instructed Moses to make a snake and put it on a pole, so that anyone who had been bitten by the venomous snakes could look at it and live (Num. 21:6–9). For several hundred years, that same bronze snake became a sacred reminder to God's people, but eventually that sacred reminder turned into an idol. King Hezekiah decided to put an end to their misguided worship and broke that snake into pieces.

Sometimes as God's children we can make idols out of things that once had special meaning. Some have done it with the cross. We don't worship the cross but the One who hung on the cross. Don't lose sight of the message of the cross.

"Just as Moses lifted up the snake in the desert, so the Son of Man must be lifted up, that everyone who believes in him may have eternal life" (John 3:14–15).

Don't worship things—worship God!

WEEK 30—TUESDAY

> *"And some of the parts that seem weakest and least important are really the most necessary. Yes, we are especially glad to have some parts that seem rather odd!" I Corinthians 12:22–23 TLB*

The Church is made up of some really odd characters . . . and you might be one of them. You've got your introverts and extroverts, personalities who can rub others the wrong way, those who are high-maintenance and those who sing off-key, those who are still changing their vocabulary since being saved, and those who will step on your toes in a very spiritual manner. We really have some parts that seem rather odd. That is how God designed us to be!

God does not want His Church to all be the same. That would be totally boring; yet, in our attempt to create unity, we want everyone to act and be the same. Sameness is not oneness. When a redeemed group of odd people comes together in the name of Jesus, great things can happen.

You are a very necessary part of the Church. Don't ever forget it—even if you are a little odd.

"When I was a child, I talked like a child, I thought like a child, I reasoned like a child. When I became a man, I put the ways of childhood behind me." I Corinthians 13:11 NIV84

You can't become a man unless you've first been a child. Children are cute, and it's fun watching them go through their growing seasons. Maturity takes longer for some than others, but there comes that moment when we have to put on our big-boy pants. If you know what I mean!

Thank God for churches, where we can be fed with the Word of God, but you must also learn how to feed yourself. Whining and crying are to be expected from children, but as we grow into spiritual adulthood, we've got to put the selfish ways of childhood behind us. There come those moments in our relationship with Jesus when we've got to start showing maturity.

God wants us to be childlike in our relationship with Him but not childish.

Put on your big-boy pants and take responsibility for your spiritual growth.

WEEK 30—THURSDAY

"Your attitude should be the same as that of Christ Jesus." Philippians 2:5 NIV84

It was halftime during one of my high school basketball games. We were losing by a large margin and our coach was furious with us for our lack of effort. After he had finished scolding us, I opened my mouth and tried to defend my attitude. Big mistake! He looked at me and said, "Roth, you're the worst of the bunch. I know you, and all that you are doing is running up and down the court. You are just going through the motions, and your attitude stinks." Ouch! That was more than fifty years ago, but I still remember it.

That can happen in the Church as well. We have those moments when we are just going through the motions with a poor attitude. What we need is an attitude adjustment.

Our attitude should be the same as that of Christ Jesus, who was motivated by sacrifice, service, and humility. The attitude behind our actions gives meaning to what we do. Is it time for an attitude check?

By the way, we still lost the game, but I had a much better attitude.

WEEK 30–FRIDAY

> *"Make every effort to keep the unity of the Spirit through the bond of peace." Ephesians 4:3 NIV84*

In order for the Church to accomplish its mission, there needs to be a unity of the Spirit, but that takes effort.

Satan loves to sow disunity among Christians. He doesn't care if we meet, but he will do all he can to keep us from being united in Christ. That's why he creates scenes within the Church: brothers and sisters in Christ who offend one another and then stop talking to each other; people who hold grudges and glare out the side of their eyes at others— during the worship service; people who avoid reconciliation because of pride. We have already been given unity in Christ—we must make an effort to keep it, preserve it, and guard it.

True unity sends a message to a broken and lost world: though we are different, we can still be one in Christ. Satan knows what the united Body of Christ can accomplish, so we must make every effort to keep it. You've got to want it!

Paul commands the Ephesians to keep the unity of the Spirit, not establish it.

Catching the Moments

What moments stand out to you from this past week?

What verse of Scripture was important to you during the past week?

In seven words or fewer, describe this past week.

_____

_____

_____

_____

_____

_____

_____

_____

_____

_____

_____

WEEK 31—SUNDAY

"He sends his word and melts them." Psalm 147:18 NIV84

Oliver Cromwell was a political leader in the British Empire during the 1600s. At one point the government had a shortage of silver, so he sent some men to the cathedral to see if they could find any. The committee of men returned and reported that the only silver they found was in the statues of the saints who were standing in the corners of the cathedral. Cromwell immediately replied, "Good. Let's melt down the saints and put them into circulation."

That's some good advice for today's Church. All too often, the living saints in our congregations are standing in the corners of the cathedral. What God needs is for us to be melted down and put back into circulation.

May the Spirit of God fall afresh on us. May He melt us and mold us and put us into circulation within His kingdom. Saints who have been melted through a refining process become far more valuable than those who stand in the corner of a cathedral.

Lord, put me back into circulation.

WEEK 31—MONDAY

"The prayer of a righteous man is powerful and effective." James 5:16b NIV84

On a recent visit to the doctor, I was waiting (in the second waiting room) for him to see me. In the room next to me was a baby who was crying from the time I sat down. After I had listened to this poor baby sob for ten straight minutes, I reached out my hand toward the next room and said out loud, "Father, in the name of Jesus, bring relief and comfort to that child." Immediately the baby stopped crying and began to laugh. I was blown away. Thank You, Lord.

We need to grab hold of the promise that the prayer of a righteous man and woman are powerful and effective. It's not our righteousness but His that makes the difference. God can change the course of someone's life just by us praying for them.

We have the incredible privilege of praying in the name of Jesus. When we do, we won't always see immediate results, but it will always bring God into the situation.

The Lord wants you to see your prayers as powerful and effective.

WEEK 31—TUESDAY

> *"Jesus said to her, 'You are right when you say you have no husband. The fact is, you have had five husbands, and the man you how have is not your husband. What you have said is quite true.'" John 4:17–18 NIV84*

In His conversation with this Samaritan woman, Jesus told her about her dark past in a few sentences. That is what some people would call an awkward moment. Jesus's honesty in that moment caused this woman to be transformed into a believer, and her testimony would later bring salvation to her whole town.

We often avoid awkward moments in the Church. But the truth of the matter is this: I'd rather someone feel awkward for a moment and then be changed than to avoid any awkwardness and stay the same. I've even heard some pastors say that they do not want to put anyone in an awkward situation. Sometimes we have to, as long as we do it with gentleness and respect.

I thank God for those awkward moments in my life when I was forced to deal with something that I would have normally avoided.

Jesus, be Lord of any awkward moments today.

WEEK 31—WEDNESDAY

"This is what the Lord says: Put your house in order, because you are going to die; you will not recover." 2 Kings 20:1 NIV 84

Isaiah the prophet delivered this powerful word to King Hezekiah. After Hezekiah prayed, God not only healed him but added fifteen years to his life. Our prayers never change God's mind, but prayer is intended to change us. This is a powerful section of Scripture that contains many items to discuss. I'll leave that up to you but will give you some items to think about:

- Would you like to know the exact date when you will die?

- If it were possible for you to know you had fifteen more years to live, would you live your life any differently?

- Are you afraid of dying?

- Put your house in order, because one day you will die.

To put our house in order means that we must take responsibility for all that God has placed in our care. Are your house and assets designated to be passed along to those survivors you have chosen?

Put your house in order before you die.

WEEK 31—THURSDAY

"Where no oxen are, the trough is clean; But much increase comes by the strength of the oxen." Proverbs 14:4 NKJV

Oxen can be expensive and time-consuming to have around. They eat a lot and require a lot of attention. Bottom line, having oxen around can be messy, but they get the work done.

Some people want a ministry to be neat and tidy. They want a place where they can come and relax and hear a good sermon, sing a few good hymns, and leave without any mess. They will spend money on building bigger troughs, but they want them to remain clean.

Thank God for the "oxen" within the Church. They can be expensive and leave a mess, but if they are doing the work, souls are being won.

We need "much increase" within the Church. We need an increase of people coming to believe in Jesus Christ as their Lord and Savior. We need more people to be saved. That will require work, and sometimes it can get messy.

What would you rather have, a clean trough or an increase?

WEEK 31–FRIDAY

"But even the archangel Michael, when he was disputing with the devil about the body of Moses, did not dare to bring a slanderous accusation against him, but said, 'The Lord rebuke you!'" Jude 9 NIV84

This story is not found in Scripture but is recorded in the apocryphal book titled *The Assumption of Moses.* In this book we are told that the task of burying Moses's body was given to Michael. The devil was said to dispute with Michael over who should have possession of Moses's remains. If that is true, what a scene that had to be.

I believe Jude's emphasis is to address the issue of rebuking the devil. William Barclay said it best: "If the greatest of good angels refused to speak evil of the greatest of the evil angels, even in circumstances like that, then surely no human being may speak evil of any angel."

While Jesus gave us authority over the devil and demons, we cannot attack those spiritual forces in our own power.

If the archangel Michael found it sufficient to say to the devil "The Lord rebuke you," it should be sufficient for us as well.

Catching the Moments

What moments stand out to you from this past week?

What verse of Scripture was important to you during the past week?

In seven words or fewer, describe this past week.

> *"Thus says the Lord: 'Make this valley full of ditches.'" 2 Kings 3:16 NKJV*

Three kings and their armies were in desperate need of a blessing. They were stuck in the middle of a desert and they called upon the Prophet Elisha to inquire of the Lord. God told them that He was going to fill their valley with pools of water, but first they had to dig some ditches to hold the blessing. "This is an easy thing in the eyes of the Lord." (v. 18). So even though it didn't rain, the next morning the ditches were flowing with water. It was their obedience to dig ditches that prepared the way for them to be blessed.

God always loves to bless us. But sometimes He needs us to "dig some ditches." Without the ditches, there would be nothing to hold the blessing when it comes. The blessing you need may seem impossible, but this is an easy thing in the eyes of the Lord.

Prepare to be blessed. Go out and dig some ditches.

> *"With God all things are possible." Matthew 19:26*

> *"Finally, brothers, good-by. Aim for perfection." 2 Corinthians 13:11 NIV84*

Matt Emmons was a participant in the 2004 Olympics. His sport was the 50-meter three-position rifle event. With a gold medal almost in hand, all he had to do was hit his final target. He didn't even have to get a bull's-eye. As he approached the target he paused and shot . . . bull's-eye! But wait, something was terribly wrong. While he hit the bull's-eye, he was focused on the wrong target. His station was in Lane 2, but he aimed at the target in Lane 3. Matt ended up finishing in eighth place.

Paul instructed the Corinthians to aim for perfection. That doesn't mean we will be perfect, but we just need that perfect standard to aim for: Jesus Christ. He knows you will not always hit the bull's-eye. Just make sure you are aiming at the right target. If you are aiming at the wrong target, it doesn't matter how accurate you are.

"Aim at heaven and you get earth thrown in. Aim at earth and you get neither."—C. S. Lewis

---

WEEK 32—TUESDAY

"For you have been granted [the privilege] for Christ's sake, not only to believe and confidently trust in Him, but also to suffer for His sake." Philippians 1:29 AMP

I stand in awe of martyrs and those who suffer for the sake of Christ. I've never had to suffer in Jesus's name—yes, I've been inconvenienced but never suffered. I once watched a video of a Christian pastor in Africa who had been beaten, had his church burned to the ground, and had his wife killed . . . just because he was a believer in Jesus Christ. He felt sorry for those who had never had the privilege of suffering for the sake of Christ.

Martyrdom is not something I pray for, but what if I were put in a position where I had to deny Jesus or be beaten? I pray that God's grace would be supplied in abundance. We have been granted the privilege to suffer for the sake of Christ.

"You're blessed when your commitment to God provokes persecution. The persecution drives you even deeper into God's kingdom." (Matthew 5:10 MSG)

"So give your servant a discerning heart to govern your people and to distinguish between right and wrong." I Kings 3:9 NIV84

As leaders in God's Church we need His wisdom to make choices. Sometimes we have to think things through and ask the Lord for discernment. Read the following statements and ask yourself if they are true or false.

- Leaders do not have to prove to others that God is guiding them.

- Leaders cannot demand respect. They can only earn it.

- The end does not justify the means in God's kingdom.

- Godly leaders will never offend the people they lead.

- Spiritual leaders should be directed by the Holy Spirit, not by their own agendas.

- Mediocrity is acceptable in the Church.

- God expects more from the pastor of a church than he does an usher.

- Leaders in the Church should all have the same temperaments and personalities.

- Character outweighs competency when it comes to leadership.

How did you do? Ask someone else how they would answer.

WEEK 32—THURSDAY

"I praise you because I am fearfully and wonderfully made."
Psalm 139:14 NIV84

I think of myself as an introvert, because that is who God created me to be. I don't have the gift of gab, I usually avoid big crowds, and I tend to recharge by being alone. Some people can get renewed by being around lots of people, but not me. Sometimes people misunderstand my shyness as being aloof, but those who know me the best accept me for who I am.

When I function within my role as a pastor, the Holy Spirit helps me come out of my comfort zones so that my introverted tendencies are not as obvious. I used to be apologetic for being introverted until I accepted who God made me to be. I also realized that there are many other introverted pastors. None of us are exclusively an introvert or extrovert, but we all tend to lean one way or another when we get out of the pulpit.

I am fearfully and wonderfully made by my God. Don't judge me if I sit off to the side at a party; I'm just getting recharged.

WEEK 32—FRIDAY

"Better is a dinner of herbs where love is, Than a fatted calf with hatred." Proverbs 15:17 NKJV

Years ago we had a teenage girl from church over to our house for dinner. She was a sweet young lady who loved the Lord but had been raised in a totally dysfunctional household. As we sat around the dinner table enjoying the food and conversation, our young visitor said, "This is really good." I thought she was talking about the food, but she was referring to the loving fellowship of just sitting around the dinner table. She had never had such an experience in her whole life. Wow!

Sitting down to dinner is a habit that is quickly being forgotten. Your household doesn't need to be poor in order to be dysfunctional. Sometimes affluent families are even more dysfunctional.

Sitting around the dinner table as a loving family will not solve all your problems, but it is one small way that you can connect with your family in your busy schedule.

Don't take the dinner table for granted!

WEEK 32–SATURDAY

Catching the Moments

What moments stand out to you from this past week?

What verse of Scripture was important to you during the past week?

In seven words or fewer, describe this past week.

_____

_____

_____

_____

_____

_____

_____

WEEK 33—SUNDAY

"Whether you turn to the right or to the left, your ears will hear a voice behind you, saying, 'This is the way; walk in it.'"
Isaiah 30:21 NIV84

Have you ever heard a voice behind you say, "This is the way; walk in it"? (I'm not talking about your wife.)While I have never heard the audible voice of God, His voice has often whispered those words to me. Whether we're looking for a parking space or doing a prayer walk, our Awesome God is able to give us specific instructions in our walk with Him.

Even Jesus said in John 10:27, "My sheep listen to my voice; I know them, and they follow me." It would be to our advantage to pay more attention to the still, small voice of the Holy Spirit who dwells within us.

More than ever before, we need the Lord's guidance in our daily walk. Trust Him to guide you today at work, at home, or in ministry.

Don't overthink this! Just try it and see where the Lord takes you today.

WEEK 33—MONDAY

"He heals the brokenhearted and binds up their wounds."
Psalm 147:3 NIV84

Doctors often prescribe antibiotics for people who have an open wound. If it remains untreated, it could easily become infected. The same is true for those who have experienced some wounds to the heart. Not your physical heart but your innermost soul that has been injured and left you brokenhearted. If left untreated, it could become infected. The answer is not antibiotics; rather you need some TLC from the Great Physician, who is able to bind up your wounds.

I have found that the best thing to do when we suffer with a broken heart is to talk it through with the Lord. Thinking about it is not enough; we've got to get alone with God and tell him how we are feeling. Even though He already knows, something special happens when we can "talk it out." It's also good to tell someone else. It doesn't have to be a professional counselor; it just needs to be someone who can hear you out and offer you some healing words of encouragement.

Talk it out with God!

WEEK 33—TUESDAY

"There is one body." Ephesians 4:4 NIV84

I love the denomination that I've grown up in and ministered in for decades. It's where I came to know my Savior and Lord, Jesus Christ. However, it saddens me when we think God favors our denomination over all the others. I've heard more than one pastor mock those believers who belong to a different denomination or, even worse, those who are part of no denomination. That type of "spiritual elitism" hinders the work of the Holy Spirit. Can you imagine our Savior saying, "Those Lutherans, they are my favorites. They really got it right"?

There is one Body of Christ, and I'm thankful that God has graciously allowed me to be part of it. I don't agree with all the doctrine of other denominations, but we share the same Head, Jesus Christ. We don't go to heaven because we are a Lutheran, Baptist, Pentecostal, or Assembly of God. We are saved by the atoning and redemptive work of our One Lord, Jesus Christ. Lutherans, when we get to heaven, we are going to have to fellowship with Baptists. Better start embracing them as brothers and sisters now.

Jesus does not have many bodies. He has **one.**

> *"Today, if you hear his voice, do not harden your hearts."*
> *Hebrews 4:7 NIV84*

Let me share with you a very sad story. Joe (not his real name) started coming to church with his wife and returned week after week, and God got his attention. When he began coming, he was in need of a new kidney; but after a couple months of Sunday mornings, the Lord healed him. Unknown to the rest of us, he continued a life of deceit, which caused him to separate from his wife and children. Eventually, he decided to come back to the Lord and chose to be baptized in our temporary summer pool set up in the churchyard. He showed up reluctantly with a cane because of a torn meniscus in his knee. It was so bad we had to help him in and out of the pool. The next morning he woke up with his knee totally healed.

The last I have heard, his heart was still hard. But the Good News is Joe is still loved by Jesus, and grace can still turn his life around. I pray that he doesn't wait too long.

Do you know any "Joes"?

> *"For the wages of sin is death, but the gift of God is eternal life*
> *in Christ Jesus our Lord." Romans 6:23 NIV84*

We have been given a gift by God—eternal life. We can't earn it! We don't deserve it! It's a gift! Let me say it once more . . . it's a gift! When Jesus Christ died and rose again, He overcame sin, death and the devil, and He offers us that same victory simply by believing and receiving Him as our Lord and Savior.

Please ponder this one important point: eternal life is a gift, but gifts still need to be received. John 1:12 tells us, "Yet to all who did receive him, to those who believed in his name, he gave the right to become children of God." God places this incredible gift before every human being, but not everyone has received it. Can you imagine taking the time to purchase and wrap a special gift for someone you love, only for them to walk away from that gift, leaving it unopened?

Have you received the gift of eternal life? If you haven't, why not pause, pray, and receive what God has purchased for you.

WEEK 33—FRIDAY

> *"Stop and consider God's wonders." Job 37:14 NIV84*

Have you lost your sense of wonder? Children are born with it, but they sometimes lose it as they grow in adulthood. When was the last time you took the time to stare at the stars in the sky and try to reach out and touch them? When was the last time you smelled a rose and allowed the aroma to fill your nostrils? When was the last time you watched an ant do amazing feats? *Stop!* Consider God's wonders around you!

I love watching the videos of color-blind people putting on those specially designed glasses that allow them to see color for the first time. Adults who have lived their whole life unable to see reds, greens, purples, and blues are brought to tears as they put on these glasses. Wonder, isn't it great?

One afternoon during our first spring in Texas, I drove by a field with acres upon acres of bluebonnets. I had to stop and look. Why hadn't I seen that before?

Stop and consider a Savior hanging on the cross for your sins. Wow!

Catching the Moments

What moments stand out to you from this past week?

What verse of Scripture was important to you during the past week?

In seven words or fewer, describe this past week.

_____

_____

_____

_____

_____

_____

_____

_____

_____

_____

_____

_____

_____

> *"Let perseverance finish its work so that you may be mature and complete, not lacking anything." James 1:4 NIV84*

My first official hospital visit as an elder was a unique experience. I was in my early thirties and honored to serve as an elder at the congregation where my father was pastor. He asked me to visit someone in the hospital who was in serious condition. I didn't stay long. I prayed and found my way to the elevator because the atmosphere was a bit overwhelming. As I stepped into the elevator, I nearly passed out and was helped to a chair when we reached the first floor. After a few minutes, I felt fine, but my spiritual ego had taken a blow.

My first experience with someone else's trauma as an elder caused "this great man of God" to nearly pass out. My dad's response: "Hey, you've got to start someplace. It will be better next time." He said the same thing after I bombed my first sermon. Dad didn't lose confidence in me.

God's gifts need time to mature. Don't let weakness or failure prevent you from moving forward in your gifts.

Let perseverance finish its work.

> *"To these four young men God gave knowledge and understanding of all kinds of literature and learning." Daniel 1:17 NIV84*

While it was God who gave Daniel and his friends knowledge and understanding, they must have had a desire to learn. All of us have had to sit through courses we did not like in order to obtain a passing grade, but God wants us to become students of life and never to stop learning. He created us to find fulfillment in gaining more knowledge and understanding—not just in Scripture but also in all kinds of literature and learning.

I regret that I never fully applied myself as a student in my early years, but I have found deep fulfillment in becoming a student of the Word in adulthood. I have also enjoyed learning how to strip furniture, play the guitar, and cook a good steak.

Never stop learning. Learn how to become a student of the Word and a student of life. May you allow the Holy Spirit to give you a hunger for knowledge and understanding.

Read a book!

WEEK 34–TUESDAY

> *"Coming over to us, he took Paul's belt, tied up his own hands and feet with it and said, 'The Holy Spirit says, in this way the Jews of Jerusalem will bind the owner of this belt and will hand him over to the Gentiles.'" Acts 21:11 NIV84*

Sometimes God chooses to use visual aids to emphasize His message. Once, while preparing for Sunday's message, the Lord led me to preach the entire sermon in handcuffs. The purpose for my bondage was to emphasize how many of us were living our lives *shackled*. While I wasn't sure if this action was truly inspired of the Lord, I went ahead and asked one of our men (a policeman) to bring his handcuffs to church with him on Sunday. He was "blown away" by my request because the Lord had just told him to bring his handcuffs.

We were both excited that we had heard the same thing from the Lord.

On Sunday, when my friend released me from my bondage at the end of the sermon, Jesus released others from theirs.

Has anyone ever confirmed what you thought the Lord was saying to you?

WEEK 34—WEDNESDAY

> *"Everything touching the water of this river shall live."*
> *Ezekiel 47:9 TLB*

I saved a life today . . . the life of a turtle. We have a pond in the park across the street from us, and there are some large turtles that make their home there. This morning I found one of them about one hundred yards from the pond, barely moving under a small tree. I put him into a bucket and carried him back to the pond. He sat motionless in the water at the edge of the pond for about thirty seconds and then miraculously came back to life and quickly returned to the fellowship of the pond. All I had to do was get my friend back in the water.

I know some of my friends have wandered far from the Living Water found in God's kingdom and have become dry and lifeless. They've had plenty of people tell them they are in the wrong place, but what they need is someone to get them back in the water. If they will only touch the water of the Holy Spirit, they will live and return to the fellowship.

Thank You, God, for the fellowship of the pond.

WEEK 34—THURSDAY

> *"I know that my Redeemer lives, and that in the end he will stand on the earth." Job 19:25 NIV84*

I love that great Easter hymn written by Samuel Medley in 1775 "I Know That My Redeemer Lives." Every verse is so meaningful, but I will only share the first one:

I know that my Redeemer lives; What comfort this sweet sentence gives!

He lives, He lives, who once was dead; He lives, my ever living Head.

What inspires me even more is the text that Samuel Medley used—a text written by Job. Yes, Job was the one who said in the midst of all his suffering, "I know that my Redeemer lives, and that in the end he will stand on the earth." Thank you, Job, for helping me put things in perspective.

There are a lot of things I don't know in this pilgrimage on earth. But I know this to be absolutely true: I know Jesus Christ lives today, and one day He is coming back. What comfort this sweet sentence gives.

What was true in 1775 is also true today.

WEEK 34–FRIDAY

> *"Benaiah son of Jehoiada, a valiant fighter from Kabzeel, performed great exploits. He struck down Moab's two mightiest warriors. He also went down into a pit on a snowy day and killed a lion." 2 Samuel 23:20 NIRV*

Benaiah was a powerful man of God. A coupleof the things we know about him are that he was chosen to be one of David's mighty men and was even in charge of David's security. You didn't mess with Benny, because it says that he struck down two of Moab's mightiest warriors. Not just any warriors; KJV translates them as "lionlike men." And the thing he is probably most known for is that he jumped into a pit (on a snowy day) and killed a lion. Eventually he became the commander in chief of Solomon's army. He was truly a mighty man of God.

When you are anointed with the Lord's power, you are able to jump into pits and kill lions and do some serious "spiritual warfare."

God needs some more mighty men who are willing to manup.

God, let Your power fall on the men in Your Church.

Catching the Moments

What moments stand out to you from this past week?

What verse of Scripture was important to you during the past week?

In seven words or fewer, describe this past week.

_____

_____

_____

_____

_____

_____

_____

_____

_____

_____

_____

_____

WEEK 35–SUNDAY

"I tell you, even though he will not get up and give you the bread because of friendship, yet because of your shameless audacity he will surely get up and give you as much as you need." Luke 11:8 NIRV

We need some more shameless audacity in our prayer life. That means we are not ashamed to keep on asking the Lord about a specific need. In this parable the persistent person was given as much bread as he needed because he kept on coming to his friend's house—even at midnight.

Please understand that our shameless audacity does not wear God down until He relents and gives us what we ask. The parable is not about changing God; it's about changing us.

We are a people who give up too easily, but God wants us to learn how to ask, and keep on asking in our prayer life ("ask and keep on asking and it will be given to you" Luke 11:9 AMP).

Shameless audacity is a quality that we need to understand more.

Maybe we don't need more faith but more audacity.

WEEK 35–MONDAY

"Therefore, there is now no condemnation for those who are in Christ Jesus." Romans 8:1 NIV84

We've all done things that we have regretted, and sometimes they can leave you in great anguish. Think of Moses, who had killed a man; David, who committed adultery and murder; and Peter, who denied Jesus. These men could have buried themselves in regret and lived under constant condemnation.

Satan is good at condemning us and filling us with regret. He knows that if we live under condemnation, we are not effective in our ministry.

Jesus Christ hung on the cross for your regret. Embrace His forgiveness and walk in the redemption He purchased for you at the cross. He doesn't condemn you, so repent, give Him your regret, and move on. We can't go back and change the past, but we can learn from it.

For those of us who believe in Jesus as our personal Lord and Savior, there is no guilty verdict and no punishment for our sinful ways. Regret does not have to control you.

Isn't grace incredible?

WEEK 35—TUESDAY

> *"He who finds a wife finds what it is good and receives favor from the Lord." Proverbs 18:22 NIV84*

God has been good to me. He has given me a wonderful wife and plenty of His favor to go with her. We are different in many ways, but our common bond is Jesus. He is the One who makes our love for each other long and lasting, and helps us persevere. I am so thankful for Alison.

We stopped trying to change each other and have begun to appreciate that fact that God "wired" us differently. We help each other through discouraging times and support each other during the encouraging times. To this day, we still have disagreements and are learning how to improve in our marital roles, but we never lose hope. We have received favor from the Lord for more than four decades, and we are blessed. One day death will separate us, but God's favor will continue.

God has been good to me. I need to tell my wife and show my love by how thankful I am.

Husbands, love and cherish your wives!

WEEK 35—WEDNESDAY

"If you declare with your mouth, 'Jesus is Lord,' and believe in your heart that God raised him from the dead, you will be saved." Romans 10:9 NIV84

Robert was Alison's brother who spent the last several months of his life living with us. God had delivered him from his addiction to drugs, but his use of unclean needles resulted in him being infected with AIDS. We loved Robert, but he always seemed to give Alison a hard time about her faith in Jesus. He never came out and confessed his belief in Jesus and always seemed to avoid the topic when it got too personal.

Several weeks before he died, he wanted Alison to see a ribbon that had been hidden in one of his books. It was the ribbon he received from a church as a child when he asked Jesus to come into his heart. Tears of joy filled our house.

As Robert faced death, he finally declared what he really believed. He died with the peace and assurance that his sins had been forgiven and he had an eternal home in heaven.

Don't ever give up on your loved ones.

WEEK 35—THURSDAY

"Which of you fathers, if your son asks for a fish, will give him a snake instead? Or if he asks for an egg, will give him a scorpion? If you then, though you are evil, know how to give good gifts to your children, how much more will your Father in heaven give the Holy Spirit to those who ask him?" Luke 11:11–13 NIV84

Why are we afraid to ask for the power of the Holy Spirit? Very often, it's fear! *What if I started acting crazy and rolling around on the ground, or what if I should start talking in tongues?*

If Jesus told us that we don't have to be afraid, then we don't have to be afraid. There are a few things we need to prioritize:

1. Jesus said we *need* the power of the Holy Spirit to be His witnesses.

2. The Holy Spirit will never harm you, only help you.

3. Stop your hesitation. Ask the Lord to fill you with the power of the Holy Spirit. Today!

4. God is not going to give you a snake or a scorpion. He is going to give you power you will never regret.

Lord, fill me with the power of Your Holy Spirit. Don't hold back!

WEEK 35–FRIDAY

> *"And you will again see the distinction between the righteous and the wicked, between those who serve God and those who don't." Malachi 3:18 NIV84*

Sometimes it is hard to make a distinction between those who are Christians and those who are not. One of the defining moments in my spiritual walk occurred in my early twenties. I was at work and one of the other employees found out that I was a Christian. They told me, "Oh, my gosh. I had no idea that you were a Christian." Their comment was extremely convicting because I realized that my life showed no proof that I was a follower of Christ.

If Jesus Christ has transformed our lives, then others should eventually see the fruit of it. That doesn't mean we have to always be talking about Jesus, but it should be reflected in how we live our lives.

As we get closer to Christ's return, the prophet Malachi said there would be a clear distinction between those who are believers and those who are not.

Lord, help others see that distinction in my life today.

Catching the Moments

What moments stand out to you from this past week?

What verse of Scripture was important to you during the past week?

In seven words or fewer, describe this past week.

_____

_____

_____

_____

_____

_____

_____

_____

_____

> *"For the mouth speaks what the heart is full of." Matthew 12:34 NIRV*

Jesus went on to say in the next verse that "A good man brings good things out of the good stored up in him, and an evil man brings evil things out of the evil stored up in him." All of us have moments when we have some things stored up in our hearts that we would prefer others not discover. The longer they stay in our hearts, the more likely they are to come out through our mouths. Most of the time, I can appear very spiritual if I just keep my mouth shut.

What is your heart full of? If it is evil, the best thing to do is repent and ask God for His forgiveness. Then you need to start filling it with good things. Read His Word and let His promises take root in your heart. When your heart is full, it will eventually come out through your mouth. Our words are powerful.

> *"For by your words you will be acquitted, and by your words you will be condemned."(Matt. 12:37)*

WEEK 36—MONDAY

> *"All hard work brings a profit, but mere talk leads only to poverty." Proverbs 14:23 NIV84*

Labor Day is a holiday that takes place on the first Monday of each September. For many people, they see this holiday as the last day of summer vacation before the start of a new school season. But this is actually a day on which we honor the working men and women in the U. S. and Canada. While there is no perfect working environment, we thank God for the improvements that have been made over the years.

Thank God for the ability to work. While it is always nice to receive a paycheck, there is an inner satisfaction just to be working. Too often we see work as a consequence of our fallen, sinful nature. Not true. God instructed Adam to work the Garden of Eden—while still living in the perfect state of His creation (Gen. 2:15).

If you are physically able to work, thank the Lord you are able. If you are limited as to what you can do, find something to occupy your mind.

There is a fulfillment that God gives to us in a job well done.

WEEK 36–TUESDAY

> *"Everyone who wants to live a godly life in Christ Jesus will be persecuted." 2 Timothy 3:12 NIV84*

I want to live a godly life so that Christ might shine through me. I cannot live such a life in my own power. I can only do it when I die to self and allow Christ to live in me and through me. When that happens I become an effective tool in ministry. I can also expect to be spiritually attacked. The Amplified Version says that those who want to live a godly life "will meet with persecution [will be made to suffer because of their religious stand]."

I am always humbled by those Christians who are severely persecuted because of the Gospel. I've never had to endure such persecution; at worst, I've had to endure some ridicule from other people.

My father had been one of my best mentors in the ministry. I once went to him and vented on how badly I was being treated in my ministry. He told me that when I am doing the godly thing, there will always be those who oppose me, but I will also be tremendously blessed.

Do you want to live a godly life?

WEEK 36—WEDNESDAY

"All my fellow townsmen know that you are a woman of noble character." Ruth 3:11 NIV84

These were the words spoken by Boaz to his soon-to-be wife, Ruth. This wonderful woman of God, who was named in the genealogy of Jesus, had developed a character that others respected.

We live in a society where many people are more concerned about their image than their character. Image is who we appear to be to others; character is who we are when nobody's looking. Image says to other people, "Like me"; character says, "Trust me." Image longs to please people; character longs to please God.

It's easy to point the finger at Hollywood and politics as being overly concerned with their image, but it happens in the Church too. I've heard of some pastors who have hired "image consultants" so they will be more appealing to their audience.

The Church needs people with good character who will be willing to make godly decisions in their personal lives as well as their ministry.

We need more leaders who we can trust more than we like.

WEEK 36—THURSDAY

"[And I pray that you] may have power, together with all the saints, to grasp how wide and long and high and deep is the love of Christ." Ephesians 3:18 NIV84

While Alison and I were once aboard a cruise to Bermuda, the captain would occasionally address the passengers with details of our location, speed, weather, etc. On one occasion he even gave us the depth of the ocean beneath us—fifteen thousand feet. I found that to be incredible!

I remember saying to Alison, "Now that's deep!" The ocean is so deep in parts that we can't even explore it.

Do you know what else is so deep that it's impossible to humanly comprehend? The love of Christ! But with the help of the Holy Spirit, we can grasp its depth (little by little). Jesus Christ came to die in our place. He died for people who didn't deserve His sacrifice and then loved us anyway. That's deep!

"Neither height nor depth . . . will be able to separate us from the love of God that is in Christ Jesus our Lord." (Roman 8:39). That's deep!

WEEK 36–FRIDAY

"God is our refuge and strength, an ever present help in trouble." Psalm 46:1 NIV84

On September 14, 2001, three days after the events of 9/11, I accompanied someone to the Armory in lower Manhattan in an attempt to locate a family member. As I walked down crowded Lexington Avenue, I was overcome with emotion by an eerie sense of silence. Already thousands of pictures of missing people lined the street. People were gentle, caring, and compassionate—not a common trait in the Big Apple. It's still easy to remember.

- Remember the awesomeness of God. Don't forget where God has brought you from—and what He has brought you through.

- Remember what is important in life.

- Remember that we are products of the past, but we don't have to be prisoners of it.

- Remember those events that brought us to our knees.

- Remember that in the midst of any normal day, tragedy can come.

- Remember that God is still our refuge and strength.

May the Holy Spirit help us to neither forget the events of 9/11 nor be in bondage to them.

Catching the Moments

What moments stand out to you from this past week?

What verse of Scripture was important to you during the past week?

In seven words or fewer, describe this past week.

_____

_____

_____

_____

_____

_____

_____

_____

_____

"News about him spread all over Syria, and people brought to him all who were ill with various diseases, those suffering severe pain, the demon-possessed, those having seizures, and the paralyzed; and he healed them." Matthew 4:24 NIV84

I want you to pay special attention to the people who were brought to Jesus. It wasn't the prim and proper, neat and clean individuals but those who were sick, diseased, and demon-possessed. In short, people with issues were brought to Him, and He healed them. That's how the kingdom of God is built—making sick people well.

Most congregations want more people to be drawn to them. When we lift up the name of Jesus, people will come and others will be brought. But who are you expecting to show up?

The Church needs to be a place where sick people can come and get well. God will do the healing and the changing. All that He expects from us is to love and pray for those people He brings. Jesus didn't come for the healthy; He came for the sick.

He did not come to call the righteous, but sinners (Matthew 9:12).

WEEK 37—MONDAY

"Accept one another, then, just as Christ accepted you, in order to bring praise to God." Romans 15:7 NIV84

During the last year of my dad's life, he had to spend some time in rehab at a nursing home. It was difficult for this strong and independent man to stay encouraged in that environment. I did my best to try and keep him focused, so I asked him to tell me some of the most important things he had learned in ministry. Right after I asked that question, an aide walked into his room and spoke to him in a very harsh tone. After she left the room, Dad turned to me and said, "Don't ever stop treating others with love and respect." I was trying to help him get focused, but he did a far better job teaching me.

I've attended a lot of workshops, conferences, and Bible studies on how to become more effective in my ministry. It was all good training, but if we are not accepting others with love and respect, it is not bringing praise to God.

Accept one another—just as Christ accepted you.

WEEK 37—TUESDAY

> *"You husbands should try to understand the wives you live with, honouring them as physically weaker yet equally heirs with you of the grace of eternal life. If you don't do this, you will find it impossible to pray properly." I Peter 3:7 PHILLIPS*

Husbands, we need to treat our wives better. Although husbands and wives are "wired" differently, we must try and understand our spouses (wives, that goes for you too). God wants us to honor our wives because they are physically weaker, not lord our strength over them. Being "head of your household" does not mean "king of your castle." We are equal heirs of eternal life, and men, we need to understand that. How do we do that? Talking and communicating with each other is a good start.

Men, when we misunderstand our roles and dishonor our wives, it is going to affect your prayer life. I don't care how involved you are in church activities, the answers to your prayers will be hindered. On the other hand, when we are walking in the Spirit as husbands, your prayers will be answered.

Husbands, how is your prayer life?

WEEK 37–WEDNESDAY

"You were running a good race. Who cut in on you and kept you from obeying the truth?" Galatians 5:7 NIV84

I don't know about you, but sometimes I get distracted from the race God has called me to. I was doing so well—had a good start, was focused, was staying in step with the Spirit—and then, all of a sudden, I allowed someone else to distract me. I allowed someone else to cut in on me and keep me from obeying the Truth. I don't blame them. I blame myself, because I should have known better. Have you ever been there? I'm sure you have.

Paul told the Galatians that "the only thing that counts is faith expressing itself through love" (Gal. 5:6). They let other voices distract them.

We need to be more careful who we listen to and who we hang out with. Satan knows how to push our buttons and distract us. If you are running a good race, praise the Lord! Enjoy it and stay on course. Don't let others keep you from obeying the truth.

Stay focused!

WEEK 37–THURSDAY

"Now faith is the substance of things hoped for, the evidence of things not seen." Hebrews 11:1 KJV

Real faith is rooted in what God has said and is shown in what we do. We don't need a lot of it to move mountains; all we need is faith the size of a mustard seed. Martin Luther King Jr. once said, "Faith is taking the first step even when you don't see the whole staircase." Have you been stepping out in faith?

What is faith to me?

- Faith sees the plans of God.

- Faith sees through confusion.

- Faith is telling anxiety to be quiet as you continue your business.

- Faith does not look back; it is focused on where God is leading.

- Faith is taking God at His word.

- Faith is a confidence that God will do exactly what He has promised.

- Faith is being able to encourage someone else when you are discouraged.

- Faith is hearing God's voice over all the other voices.

What about you? What is faith to you?

WEEK 37—FRIDAY

"Be prepared in season and out of season." 2 Timothy 4:2 NIV84

When I was in my late fifties, I had both knees replaced—at the same time. I couldn't even walk around the block anymore, so I made the decision to get them both done. When the surgery was complete and I was assigned a room, my epidural had finally worn off and my pain level was getting worse.

As Alison sat by my side, we noticed a man standing in our doorway. He would occasionally glance our way but did not come in. I finally asked him to step into my room and found out that he was a new hospital chaplain—first day on the job. He was obviously quite nervous, and when he found out that I was a pastor, he asked me to pray for him. Sometimes you just have to smile.

So with my pain level approaching ten, I found myself praying for a chaplain in need.

Always be prepared to be used by the Lord—in season and out of season.

WEEK 37–SATURDAY

Catching the Moments

What moments stand out to you from this past week?

What verse of Scripture was important to you during the past week?

In seven words or fewer, describe this past week.

_____

_____

_____

_____

_____

_____

_____

_____

_____

_____

> *"Let Your mercy and loving-kindness, O Lord, be upon us, in proportion to our waiting and hoping for You." Psalm 33:22 AMP*

We all want God's mercy and loving-kindness to rest upon us. Who wouldn't? But I love how the Amplified Version puts it: "in proportion to our waiting and hoping for You." Did you catch that? If we are willing to wait and hope more in the Lord, we will discover more of His mercy and loving-kindness. I need more of that!

"Mercy" is defined as "God not giving us what we deserve." God, please don't give me what I deserve. As I wait and hope in Him, mercy is revealed. Thank You, Lord. Loving-kindness is God freely giving to us what we don't deserve. God, please give me what I don't deserve. As I wait and hope in Him, love seems to grow. Thank You, Lord.

Waiting and hoping for the Lord is a good thing. We are so incredibly blessed to have a God so full of mercy and loving-kindness.

When your faith is small yet God answers your prayer, that is **mercy.**

WEEK 38–MONDAY

> *"'What do you want me to do for you?' Jesus asked him. The blind man said, 'Rabbi, I want to see.'" Mark 10:51 NIV84*

Jesus asked blind Bartimaeus a very powerful question: "What do you want me to do for you?" Bartimaeus was not shy; he told Jesus exactly what he wanted: "I want to see!" James tells us that we may not have because we have not asked.

Jesus has not changed and is still asking us that same question today. How would you answer Him? Sometimes we get overly spiritual and think it is wrong to be too specific, so we give a very general response: "Just bless me, Lord." We may think that our personal request is not important enough when it is compared to the salvation of souls.

Friend, your needs are important to God. While He is not some heavenly ATM machine that will immediately dispense what you request, it is important to ask and you will receive.

So today how would you answer that incredible question? Tomorrow your answer could be totally different.

WEEK 38–TUESDAY

> *"Trust in the Lord and do good; dwell in the land and enjoy safe pasture." Psalm 37:3 NIV84*

Here are four words to carry with you throughout the day: Trust, Do, Dwell, and Enjoy.

- Trust in the Lord—Totally lean on and rely on Him in all your choices. He won't let you down.

- Do good—Do something for someone else in the name of Jesus. Put your faith into action. Just do it!

- Dwell in the land—Don't just take up space; put down your roots where God has placed you and *live.*

- Enjoy safe pasture—Take time to enjoy your pasture—the place where you are spiritually fed. Just as sheep enjoy a green pasture, so our Shepherd leads us to safe pastures where we can lie down and enjoy them.

Our day will go so much smoother if we just intentionally put these four words into practice.

Living out the Christian life is not difficult; it only takes simple child-like faith.

WEEK 38–WEDNESDAY

> *"Jesus said to them, 'Take off the grave clothes and let him go.'"*
> *John 11:44 NIV84*

Jesus was standing in front of the tomb of his friend Lazarus, who had been dead four days. People were crying and upset, but Jesus knew that these same people would soon see the glory of God. Jesus spoke those life-giving words, "Lazarus, come out," and the dead man came alive. Lazarus came walking out of the tomb alive but still wrapped and confined in his grave clothes. It was then He spoke a second time and told the astonished mourners to take off his grave clothes and loose him.

Jesus came into this world to bring life and freedom to those who were lost. It is only through Him that people come spiritually alive, but sometimes they are still not free because their grave clothes need to be removed. Don't judge them; help them take off their grave clothes. If Jesus has set you free, why not use your freedom to help someone else?

People are waiting to see the glory of God.

WEEK 38–THURSDAY

> *"Be diligent to know the state of your flocks, and attend to your herds." Proverbs 27:23 NKJV*

Let me address my fellow pastors. I don't know about you, but I am sometimes easily distracted, and during my weekly routine of pastoral ministry I could easily "major in the minors." What I mean is that I could find myself consumed with things that would distract me from my main calling as a pastor: taking care of sheep.

God has called us to be diligent to know the state of the flock He has assigned to us. As we follow our Good Shepherd, our first priority is to focus on the sheep—not the sheep pen or our career. It's not that sheep pens and our careers are unimportant, it's just that we sometimes disconnect with the sheep.

It's important to know what is going on in the lives of the people in your congregation. There are those who need some TLC and others who need to be encouraged to step up. There are some who need to be rescued (but would never say so) and others who need to be taught how to rescue others.

Fellow pastors, we are truly blessed.

WEEK 38–FRIDAY

"But ask the animals, and they will teach you." Job 12:7 NIV84

There are so many things that we can learn from God's creations—including all the animals.

There was a pond across the street from our first house in Texas where many ducks and turtles would gather on a regular basis. Often when we took our dog, Samson, for a walk, God seemed to speak some encouraging words through those ducks and turtles. Our Creator uses His creation to speak to His children: the eagle, ant, donkey, sparrow, lion, etc.

God once used our dog to help me understand praise and worship. Whenever we would come home, our dog was always there to joyfully greet us at the door—that's like praise. After we've been home for a while, the dog will settle down, lie at our feet, and enjoy our presence—that's like worship. That may be too simplistic for some people, but not for God.

The eagle has taught me how to soar, the ant how to stay busy, and the donkey humility.

"Ask the animals . . . they will teach you." Those are God's words, not mine.

Catching the Moments

What moments stand out to you from this past week?

What verse of Scripture was important to you during the past week?

In seven words or fewer, describe this past week.

_____

_____

_____

_____

_____

_____

_____

_____

_____

_____

_____

_____

WEEK 39—SUNDAY

"In those days Israel had no king; everyone did as they saw fit."
Judges 21:25 NIV84

Israel was in a very vulnerable position. Because they had no king, meaning they had no one they recognized as their supreme ruler, they were left to determine on their own what was right and what was wrong. What a dangerous place to be.

It is so important to recognize Jesus Christ as your King so that He might have supremacy in everything (Col. 1:18). If we don't, we will be left to determine for ourselves what is right and what is wrong.

When we declare Jesus to be our good and righteous King, that means we are willing to give Him the final authority in our decision-making. It's not that He has taken away our free will, but as subjects in His kingdom, we want to please Him. We can trust Him as our King, knowing that "not my will, but Your will" is a far better approach to live than "doing as we see fit."

Jesus "is Lord of lords and King of kings." Rev. 17:14

WEEK 39—MONDAY

"I want to know Christ—yes, to know the power of his resurrection and participation in his sufferings."
Philippians 3:10 NIRV

For more than thirty-two years of pastoral ministry at the same congregation, my wife and I were lavished with an immense amount of unconditional and sacrificial love from the members. We were blessed! While we never took their love for granted, there was a void left in our lives when we moved to Texas. To this day, we still miss the love of those wonderful people, but God has also been teaching us something very special.

When the love of others is suddenly removed from your life, it can leave a hole in your soul. But Jesus understands that. He has been teaching us some very important lessons. In His still, small voice, He seemed to say to me: "There will be others to love you in the same way, but for now, I am going to fill that void with more of Myself. I have given you this hole in your soul as a gift so that you can know Me more."

And He has been doing exactly that.

Jesus, I want to know You more intimately.

WEEK 39—TUESDAY

> *"But because my servant Caleb has a different spirit and follows me wholeheartedly, I will bring him into the land he went to, and his descendents will inherit it." Numbers 14:24 NIV84*

Caleb had a "different" spirit. It wasn't because he was perfect or better than everyone else; he just obeyed his God as others tested Him. It is not always easy to be different. When you choose not to go along with the majority, people will call you different. When other people in the Church walk in fear and you walk in faith, people will call you different.

God has called us to have a different spirit. When we live a life of love and obedience toward Jesus Christ, we may be labeled as "different," but we will also get all the blessings that God has promised.

Don't follow the Lord halfhearted. Let the Holy Spirit make you different and bring you into some blessings that you and your family will enjoy. I am so thankful to know some "Calebs." They are not better than anyone else. They just follow Jesus wholeheartedly.

A Hebrew meaning for "Caleb" is "faithful, devotion, wholehearted, bold, brave."

"Martha, Martha, you are worried and upset about many things, but only one thing is needed. Mary has chosen what is better, and it will not be taken away from her." Luke 10:42 NIV84

Martha was doing a good thing by preparing dinner for Jesus. Her problem was that she got distracted. Mary chose what was better. She chose to sit at Jesus's feet listening to Him teach. As a Christian, many of the choices we have to make are not just between good and evil. Many of our choices come down to choosing between what is good and what is better.

Like Martha, when we neglect the better things, we usually end up worried and bothered. Sitting at the feet of Jesus is a choice all of us should be making at the start of each day.

Don't let the good things in life crowd out the better things of life. That is true in our home life and also our Church life. God wants to be part of the choices we have to make.

Ask the Lord for the grace to make better choices.

WEEK 39–THURSDAY

"Brothers and sisters, if someone is caught in a sin, you who live by the Spirit should restore that person gently." Galatians 6:1 NIRV

Have you ever been caught in your own sin? It can be very humbling and embarrassing, but it can also lead to healing. Paul told the Galatians that if they are truly living by the Spirit, and catch someone else in a sin, it is their responsibility to restore that person gently. The word "restore" comes from the Greek word that refers to setting a broken bone. How we treat others in their sin reveals quite a bit about our own walk in the Spirit. To set a broken bone is usually a painful process, but if it is done correctly, it will lead to healing.

When the woman caught in adultery was brought before Jesus, He gently reset her broken spirit. He didn't condemn her but encouraged her to leave her life of sin (John 8:1–11). Ask the Lord to teach you how to restore other people gently when they are caught in sin.

Treat them as you would want to be treated.

WEEK 39–FRIDAY

> *"Moses said to Pharaoh, 'I leave to you the honor of setting the time for me to pray for you and your officials and your people that you and your houses may be rid of the frogs.'"*
> *Exodus 8:9 NIV84*

The plague of frogs upon the nation of Egypt was horrible. These slimy pests were everywhere: in the beds, ovens, and dresser drawers. It was so bad that Pharaoh asked Moses to pray to their God to remove the frogs. Moses not only said that he would pray, he left it up to Pharaoh to name the time. And do you know what Pharaoh said? Tomorrow! Why in the world would he want to live another day with the frogs when he could be free of them today? Pride and procrastination! Pharaoh put off to tomorrow what God was able to do today.

Do you have some frogs that are messing up your lives? God has given you the honor of setting the time to pray them out. Don't procrastinate.

Don't put off until tomorrow what you are able to pray about today.

Catching the Moments

What moments stand out to you from this past week?

What verse of Scripture was important to you during the past week?

In seven words or fewer, describe this past week.

_____

_____

_____

_____

_____

_____

_____

_____

_____

_____

_____

_____

"Then you will know the truth, and the truth will set you free."
John 8:32 NIV84

We know from John 14:6 that Jesus refers to Himself as the Truth. He came into this world to bring freedom to those who were held captive to the power of sin. Through His death and resurrection, He conquered the power of sin, death, and the devil, and made real freedom available to everyone who believes in Him.

Please notice in the preceding verse that it does not say *truth will set you free* but clearly says that *knowing the truth will set you free*. Do you know the truth? Do you know Jesus?

We are saved by believing that Jesus rose from the dead and confessing with our mouth that Jesus is Lord (Rom. 10:9). As we grow in our relationship and get to know Him more and hold to His teaching, we begin to experience what freedom is all about. Don't believe the lies Satan tries to plant in you.

Believe the Truth. Know the Truth. Freedom belongs to you. Jesus promised it.

WEEK 40-MONDAY

"But his delight is in the law of the Lord, and on his law he meditates day and night." Psalm 1:2 NIV84

It is very important that we not only read the Word of God but that we take time to process what we read. That means we need to spend time meditating on Scripture. Christian meditation is not a process where we empty our minds and wait for something to fill them. No, it is when we fill them with the Word of God and allow the Holy Spirit to bring meaning and understanding to what we have just read. If we find delight in gathering the information, the Spirit of God will give the revelation.

Sometimes we make the mistake of reading many chapters a day but take no time to process them.

Do what you have to do to carry the Word with you throughout the day: memorize it, write it down, take your phone, or carry your Bible.

The more we meditate on the Word of the Lord, the more we will delight in it.

WEEK 40–TUESDAY

"Delight yourself in the Lord; And He will give you the desires of your heart." Psalm 37:4 NASB

Several years ago I was experiencing tremendous pain in both of my knees. As I awaited double knee-replacement surgery, someone asked me the following question:"What are two desires of your heart?" I answered quickly.

1. I wanted to walk on the beach again with my wife. My knees had gotten so bad that I was physically unable to take that walk in the sand. In the months that followed my surgery, our congregation sent us on a trip to Bermuda. As I walked those beautiful beaches with Alison, I thanked the Lord (and Good Shepherd) for giving me a desire of my heart.

2. I wanted to go on a mission trip. About a year later I found myself in India on a life-changing mission trip. That too was paid for by Good Shepherd.

I concentrated on learning how to delight myself in the Lord, and He gave me the desires of my heart. What about you? What are the desires of your heart?

Lord, teach me how to delight myself in You.

WEEK 40-WEDNESDAY

> *"For we are to God the pleasing aroma of Christ among those who are being saved and those who are perishing." 2 Corinthians 2:15 NIRV*

There are certain smells that are very pleasing to me: the smell of a freshly brewed pot of coffee when I wake up in the morning, the smell of bacon frying in the pan, and the smell of a steak cooking on a charcoal grill. Certain aromas just bring a smile to your face.

Did you know that there are aromas that please our Heavenly Father? We are the pleasing aroma of His Son, Jesus Christ. God smelled the sacrifice of Thanksgiving that Noah offered and was pleased (Gen. 8:21). He is pleased with the fragrant offerings that come from willing hearts (Phil. 4:8). Even our prayers rise as incense before Him(Ps. 141:2).

We spend a lot of money making ourselves smell better to one another. That's good, but we should also be concerned about our spiritual scent.

Ask yourself how you are smelling to those around you. And how are you smelling to your Heavenly Father?

WEEK 40-THURSDAY

> *"At this, Job got up and tore his robe and shaved his head. Then he fell to the ground in worship . . . may the name of the Lord be praised." Job 1:20–21 NIRV*

Job was a godly man who lost everything—family, home, business, and assets—in one day. It's hard to imagine the grief he must have felt as he made arrangements to bury all his sons and daughters. After hearing one bad report after another, Job showed his grief by tearing his robe and shaving his head. Then he fell to the ground in worship. Wow!

He chose to worship God while he was overwhelmed with grief. That takes great faith. It is not all that difficult to worship God when all the blessings are flowing, but is our passion to worship still there when those blessings are taken from us?

In my opinion, those in their lowest state show the highest form of worship. I am moved by people who can still say "May the name of the Lord be praised" after they have lost virtually everything.

Praise God when blessings do not flow.

WEEK 40-FRIDAY

"He went out to the field one evening to meditate." Genesis 24:63 NIRV

Isaac purposely and intentionally went out into a field to be alone with his God. It would do us well if we would do the same thing. Even though He was always needed and being sought after, Jesus went off to be alone with His Father. It was in the moment alone that Jesus found Himself being equipped for His public ministry.

Do you set time aside just to meditate? Reading your Bible and talking to God are very important, but do you take time to just think and wonder and imagine?

I challenge you to go out into a field, park, or lake just to meditate. Leave your cell phone behind and any other convenience that may distract us from connecting with our God in private. Start by just thanking Him for His creation; take a deep breath and give yourself permission to be still.

Do you know what happened to Isaac after he went out into the field to meditate? He met his wife.

Great things can happen when you spend time alone with the Lord.

Catching the Moments

What moments stand out to you from this past week?

What verse of Scripture was important to you during the past week?

In seven words or fewer, describe this past week.

_____

_____

_____

_____

_____

_____

_____

_____

WEEK 41-SUNDAY

"Amen. Hallelujah!" Revelation 19:4 NIRV

One of the most moving worship experiences I've had occurred while I was on a mission trip to India. During the opening worship service in Agra, about fifty to sixty of us were singing a song under the leadership of one man on an electric keyboard. Then the power went out, a common occurrence in India. In the darkness of the room and with no accompaniment from the keyboard, the congregation kept right on singing. While I could not understand the lyrics to the song, I understood the chorus perfectly. They kept singing "Amen, hallelujah," over and over again. Those two words shine through any language barrier.

I was brought to tears as I sang along in this powerful, spirit-filled moment. The loss of electricity was replaced by a power straight from heaven.

What would happen if the electricity went out during one of our worship services? Would we be able to worship the Lord in darkness with no hymnal or accompaniment?

God is able to unite any group of people when they learn how to sing "Hallelujah" together under the leadership of the Holy Spirit.

WEEK 41-MONDAY

"He will punish those who do not know God and do not obey the gospel of our Lord Jesus Christ. They will be punished with everlasting destruction and shut out from the presence of the Lord." 2 Thessalonians 1:8–9 NIRV

To my knowledge, Jesus talked about hell more than He did about heaven in the Gospels. It would do us well to talk more about hell within the Church. Not for the purpose of scaring people into heaven but to give a greater urgency to the saved to pray more for their unsaved loved ones.

When people die, they will spend eternity in one of two places: heaven or hell. Many people are ignorant of what eternal separation from God will look like. They say things such as, "I'd rather go to hell and be with my friends than be in heaven with hypocrites." That's ignorance.

God never sends anyone to hell; people choose to go there on their own. Jesus Christ suffered and died to redeem us from the horrible place of darkness and suffering, and all we have to do is to reach out by faith and receive it.

There will be no answered prayers in hell.

WEEK 41–TUESDAY

"Write down the revelation and make it plain on tablets so that a herald may run with it." Habakkuk 2:2 NIV84

I'm the type of person who needs to write things down, especially when God reveals something to me. I write it down not just for the sake of passing it along to others but just to remind myself. I have my senior moments!

Before the age of television, we were very much a "word-centered" society, but over the last couple generations we have now become more of an "image-centered" society. God can use both, but there is something special about words—especially written words.

What has God been revealing to you? Write it down. What truth has the Holy Spirit revealed to you while reading the Word or communicating in prayer? Write them down! It takes thought and discipline, but remember—God has given you a spirit of self-discipline (2 Tim. 1:7).

Maybe it's time to start journaling, blogging, or just writing your own prayers.

Write it down on your tablet or PC so that others can benefit from it.

WEEK 41-WEDNESDAY

> *"As a bridegroom rejoices over his bride, so will your God rejoice over you." Isaiah 62:5 NIV84*

I still remember the day of my wedding. As I watched Alison appear and walk up the aisle of the church, my heart was pounding and my heart was excited. I was rejoicing over my bride, and have been ever since.

The Bible refers to the Church as the Bride of Christ. One day we are going to be united with our Bridegroom, and there is going to be a wedding banquet that will blow us away. Isn't it awesome to think that our Lord is going to rejoice over us as a bridegroom rejoices over his bride? We don't know when our Bridegroom will come for us, but He will be rejoicing when He does.

Our Bridegroom loves us so much that He chose to die in our place and then rose again. I can't wait to be united with Him, and He is waiting to be united with us.

That is what we have been destined for - to spend eternity with Jesus.

WEEK 41-THURSDAY

> *"My soul thirsts for God, for the living God. When can I go and meet with God?" Psalm 42:2 NIV84*

A young salesman was returning to his sales manager after blowing a big opportunity. With sorrow he told his boss, "I guess that proves that you can lead a horse to water but can't make him drink." The sales manager was quick to reply, "Son, your job is not to make the horse drink. Your job is to make the horse thirsty."

Jesus offers the world rivers of living water, and He will use the Church to deliver this water. But our job is not to make people drink the Living Water; our job is to make them thirsty. Our lives should be so filled with Christ that when others get to know us, they will become thirsty for the Gospel.

When we allow those rivers of living water to flow from our lives, many thirsty people will say like the Samaritan women (John 4:15), "Sir, give me this water." That means you have to maintain your own thirst for God.

Ask yourself: "How can my thirst for God increase?"

WEEK 41–FRIDAY

> *"Put their hope in God, who richly provides us with every-thing for our enjoyment." I Timothy 6:17 NIRV*

Four of us had been on a mission trip to Kingston, Jamaica. I was honored to preach at Barbican Baptist Church and a new parish in the hills of Golden Springs. It was a great few days. Our return flight was delayed when we got to the airport, and then we ended up waiting for more than twelve hours for the next available flight. We were all very tired, but we knew God was doing something with our delay.

Finally we boarded our flight back to NY, and to our surprise the head flight attendant was also the worship leader I sat next to on Sunday. Since first-class seats just so happened to be empty, she moved all four of us to our new seats after takeoff. We had a very comfortable three-hour ride home. I don't know who was smiling more—the four of us or God.

God provides us with everything we need, and occasionally provides us with things for our enjoyment. Isn't He incredible?

Catching the Moments

What moments stand out to you from this past week?

What verse of Scripture was important to you during the past week?

In seven words or fewer, describe this past week.

> *"The word of the Lord came to Jonah's son of Amittai: 'Go to the great city of Nineveh and preach against it . . .' but Jonah ran away." Jonah 1:1,3 NIV84*

We've all got our Nineveh! We've all got those places where our gracious and compassionate God will call us to go—places we would never choose to go on our own. Our Nineveh is not always a place we can locate on a map. It might be something that causes fear to overwhelm us; it might be a people we do not like or a task we do not want to face. Although our Ninevehs may differ, they are all equally scary.

Why did God stick with Jonah when he disobeyed his calling? God could have just as easily sent someone else. That's true, but remember this important point: God loves the messenger as much as His message.

I must admit that there have been those times when I have run away from what God called me to do, but He stuck with me.

Our God is gracious and compassionate, slow to anger, and abounding in love (4:2).

> *"Train up a child in the way he should go, And when he is old he will not depart from it." Proverbs 22:6 NKJV*

"Parents need to give their children two things: roots and wings." I've seen this quote appear on pictures, books, and illustrations. Its wording is not found in Scripture, but the truths are found throughout the Bible.

We need to train our children to have *roots*. We need to show them by example the importance of establishing a strong home life. We also have to show them how to make their own godly decisions by staying rooted in Jesus Christ and His Word.

We need to train our children to have *wings*. The time will come when your children will have to leave the safe haven of their home and need to know how to fly into the future and soar on wings as eagles. Your children not only need this important training; they also need your permission.

Giving your children roots and wings is not merely something that is taught; it is more effective when it is caught. Train by example.

WEEK 42–TUESDAY

> *"I saw heaven standing open and there before me was a white horse, whose rider is called Faithful and True. With justice he judges and wages war." Revelation 19:11 NIV84*

When Jesus made His triumphant entry into Jerusalem, He came gentle and lowly, riding on a donkey. When He comes again He will be riding a white horse. Jesus will be described as Faithful and True, with the purpose of judging and waging war. He will be dressed in a robe dipped in blood, and the armies of heaven will be following him on white horses. His eyes will be like a blazing fire, and on his robe and on his thigh will be written this name: King of Kings and Lord of Lords.

Read chapter 19 of Revelation and try to imagine what it will be like when our King of Kings and Lord of Lords comes on the scene. He will not be coming back as Little Baby Jesus, sweet and mild, resting in His manger.

Aren't you glad that you are loved and accepted by Jesus?

Our future is secure in the One who is called Faithful and True.

WEEK 42–WEDNESDAY

> *"Suppose one of you has a hundred sheep and loses one of them.*
> *Doesn't he leave the ninety-nine in the open country and go*
> *after the lost sheep until he finds it?" Luke 15:4 NIV84*

Jesus's love for us is absolutely incredible. He uses this parable to challenge us to leave the ninety-nine and go after the one lost sheep. Only the love of God would do something like that. Are we willing to leave the safety and comfort of the other sheep and go after one that is still lost? When we realize how much our God loves us, only then are we able to go out after the lost sheep.

I love the words to the chorus of "Reckless Love" by Cory Asbury:

> *Oh, the overwhelming, never-ending, reckless love of God*
> *Oh, it chases me down, fights 'til I'm found, leaves the ninety-nine*
> *I couldn't earn it, and I don't deserve it, still, You give Yourself away*
> *Oh, the overwhelming, never-ending, reckless love of God, yeah*

We need to ask the Lord to give us that type of love for the lost.

WEEK 42–THURSDAY

> *"His master replied, 'Well done, good and faithful servant!*
> *You have been faithful with a few things; I will put you in*
> *charge of many things. Come and share your master's happi-*
> *ness!'" Matthew 25:21 NIV84*

The Parable of the Talents (Matt. 25:14–30) is not a teaching about salvation by good works. It's a story about being faithful servants in God's kingdom. I may not be as gifted as some other people, but that's OK. God just wants me to be faithful with what He has given me.

When I get to heaven, I long to hear the words of my Master, "Steve, well done, good and faithful servant." By my own merits, I know that I don't deserve such a greeting, but if He trusted me enough to give me a few gifts, then I want to be faithful with them. Maybe, just maybe, He might even put me in charge of a few things in heaven.

Friends, we will get to spend eternity sharing our Master's happiness.

As for now, be faithful with what you have been given.

WEEK 42–FRIDAY

> *"He who rebukes a man will in the end gain more favor than he who has a flattering tongue." Proverbs 28:23 NIV84*

How well do you accept correction? A mark of Christian maturity is not the ability to receive compliments and words of approval but the ability to receive words of rebuke and correction *without taking offense.* Even when someone's correction is unwarranted, don't get bent out of shape. Flattery can do far more damage to our character than a friend who will give it to you straight. Who are the people in your life who have the freedom to pull no punches and tell you what you need to hear?

There are some people who think they have been given the "gift of rebuking" but will get totally bent out of shape when they are corrected. Those who have learned how to take a rebuke (without taking offense) are more effective in giving a corrective rebuke.

When God asks us to give a rebuke, don't be timid or apologetic, but do it with grace.

Never look to embarrass people but to edify them. That's what friends do.

Catching the Moments

What moments stand out to you from this past week?

What verse of Scripture was important to you during the past week?

In seven words or fewer, describe this past week.

_____

_____

_____

_____

_____

_____

_____

_____

_____

_____

_____

_____

_____

> *"[I will] not, [I will] not, [I will] not in any degree leave you helpless nor forsake nor let [you] down (relax My hold on you)! [Assuredly not!]" Hebrews 13:5 AMPC*

I love how the Amplified Classic Version translates the simple but profound promise found in Hebrews 13:5. Three times the Lord assures us—"I will not, I will not, I will not . . . leave you helpless or let you down." He adds His exclamation by saying "Assuredly not!" Whenever I have my moments when I feel helpless or forsaken, I know I'm not, because my God is with me.

When our gracious God promises to take care of us, He means it. He has never failed us, and He never will. He will not. He will not. He will not. There are so many hurting people who think that God has abandoned them, but He hasn't. When circumstances and people are against me, my God is for me. He will never relax His hold on you. Assuredly not!

He will not. He will not. He will not.

> *"And hope does not disappoint us, because God has poured out his love into our hearts by the Holy Spirit, whom he has given us." Romans 5:5 NIV84*

I once had the distinct honor of preaching at a close friend's funeral service in Harlem. Cancer had caused her to suffer greatly in her last year, and even though her faith in Jesus was strong and her life was encouraging, emotions were running high as we all mourned the loss of this great woman of God.

As I stood before the people, I was fighting back the tears. The Holy Spirit gave me the strength to begin, and the first words out of my mouth were "Grief can be messy!" We all breathed a holy sigh of agreement, and I continued with hope.

Even though we are assured of eternal life and forgiveness of sins, death has a way of causing us to evaluate our lives. We get to take a close look at our vulnerability and mortality and grieve like anyone else. Sometimes grief can be messy even for Christians, but hope does not disappoint us.

Hope in Christ keeps us anchored—enables us to grieve with hope.

WEEK 43–TUESDAY

> *"On hearing this, Jesus said, 'It is not the healthy who need a doctor, but the sick. But go and learn what this means: I desire mercy, not sacrifice. For I have not come to call the righteous, but sinners.'" Matthew 9:12–13 NIV84*

Jesus never intended His Church to be a neat and clean country club for the saints. He wanted it to be a hospital for sinners. He wants His Church to be a place where people who are sick can come and get well.

There are so many people who come from chaotic and dysfunctional households, and need a place where they can find some order and purpose. Therefore the Church should be a place for OCD (Ordered Chaotic Dysfunction). I once heard a longtime member of the Church declare, "I don't want any more of those *sinners* to come to my church." He died a few months later.

We need to rethink the reason that the Church is here. It could get messy at times, but that's what usually happens in emergency rooms.

God uses forgiven sinners to connect others sinners with Doctor Jesus.

WEEK 43-WEDNESDAY

"Do not mistreat an alien or oppress him, for you were aliens in Egypt." Exodus 22:21 NIV84

The Statue of Liberty was dedicated on October 28, 1886. At the base of this statue are inscribed the following words:

"Give me your tired, your poor, your huddled masses yearning to breathe free, the wretched refuse of your teeming shore. Send these, the homeless, tempest-tossed to me, I lift my lamp beside the golden door!"

These words are taken from a poem written by Emma Lazarus in 1883. The famous words were cast into a plaque and mounted inside the pedestal's lower level in 1903. Lady Liberty is quite an impressive sight at she stands tall in New York Harbor. She is a universal symbol of freedom and democracy.

As the heated debate over immigration continues, let us not forget what the Lord told the nation of Israel about their treatment of aliens. Do not mistreat or oppress aliens.

It is important to have laws established regarding aliens wishing to immigrate into our country, but so is the heart behind those laws.

WEEK 43-THURSDAY

"The gullible believe anything they're told." Proverbs 14:15 MSG

Sometimes we are so gullible. How many times have people posted a story on Facebook (in an attempt to appear spiritual) without knowing its source? Then we pass it along as fact. How many times has another brother or sister accepted a teaching as truth just because "Brother So-and-So" said so?

Don't believe everything you hear. How do we protect ourselves from being taken in by false teachers and false information? Study the Word!

I once heard a well-known evangelist share with a crusade that Jesus was going to physically appear at one of his future gatherings. I was appalled at how quickly the crowd believed his teaching. The Word clearly teaches that the next time we physically see Jesus will be at His Second Coming (Heb. 9:28).

Whether it is gossip or a false teaching, don't be so gullible. An ongoing study of Scripture will not only build your faith; it will also provide you with knowledge and understanding that will make you wise and discerning.

Study the Word. Know your source.

WEEK 43—FRIDAY

> *"Precious in the sight of the Lord is the death of his saints."*
> *Psalm 116:15 NIV84*

November 1is All Saints Day. This is a special day on the Church calendar on which we remember all Christian saints—especially those saints who have died and gone to be with the Lord in heaven. We do not pray *to* the dead or *for* the dead or *talk* to the dead. We remember them and give thanks for the influence they had on our lives. One day all the saints—on earth and in heaven—will be reunited and worship around the throne of God. I get exited thinking about that day.

Why aren't we more excited about heaven?

1. We think this world is our home—not heaven. We are just passing through this earth.

2. We misunderstand what heaven is like. We try and compare it to this world . . . and we can't.

3. We've got to die to get to heaven.

4. We may be unsure about our passage from earth to heaven.

Make no mistake about it—the death of God's saints is very precious to Him.

Catching the Moments

What moments stand out to you from this past week?

What verse of Scripture was important to you during the past week?

In seven words or fewer, describe this past week.

_____

_____

_____

_____

_____

_____

_____

_____

"Lord, teach us to pray." Luke 11:1 NIV84

Election Day is close, and all of us would agree that we need to pray. But here's the dilemma—I have Christian friends who have prayed and are voting for a Democratic candidate, and I also have Christian friends who have prayed and are voting for a Republican candidate. Is someone praying the wrong prayer? Here are some questions and thoughts to ponder before you vote:

- Can you embrace a brother or sister in Christ who has voted for someone different than you?

- What do you pray when neither candidate fully represents your view as a child of God?

- Will you be willing to pray for whatever person wins the election?

- Is the platform of a political party more important than the character of a candidate?

- Vote your conscience. Your vote is important and makes a difference.

- You cannot reduce the Redeemer of Mankind to fit into a political party.

When you wake up on the day after Election Day, God's purpose will not have changed.

Oh, Lord, teach us how to pray. I pray that my vote will be influenced by the Holy Spirit and not a political opinion.

WEEK 44—MONDAY

"Blessed be the name of God, forever and ever. He knows all, does all: He changes the seasons and guides history, He raises up kings and also brings them down, he provides both intelligence and discernment." Daniel 2:20–21 MSG

God is going to do something through our voting that will guide our history. There will be candidates who will be raised up and there will be others who will be brought down. Your vote counts! Even if your candidate is defeated, your vote counts!

Before you vote, take some time to seek the Lord with an open heart.

Lord, I need You to guide me as I go to the polls. I don't want to be led by a political agenda or political correctness. I want to be guided by Your Spirit. Let me cast my vote with a clear conscience. While all the candidates need an extra measure of intelligence and discernment, so do the voters. Blessed be the name of the Lord! In Jesus's name. Amen.

If your candidate wins, don't gloat. If he or she loses, don't despair. Jesus is still King!

WEEK 44—TUESDAY

"'Not by might nor by power, but by my Spirit,' says the Lord Almighty." Zechariah 4:6 NIV84

There is nothing quite as exhilarating as preaching a sermon that the Holy Spirit has anointed. There is something incredibly special about experiencing the Spirit bringing all your preparation together so that your words fall on an attentive audience and people are more impressed with God than they are the preacher. I am still amazed to see some people leave the worship service rejoicing or in tears or just more determined. It doesn't happen all the time, but when it does, it's a "rush."

When I finally get in the car and begin my ride home, there is a deep satisfaction knowing that God just used me to speak His word with clarity and boldness. *But I am quick to remember:* "That did not just happen because of my might or power. That was *all* the Spirit of God." Pride is dangerous—especially in ministry.

Lord, I long for your anointing whenever I preach or teach, but don't let my preparation or pride be an obstacle to the work of Your Spirit.

WEEK 44—WEDNESDAY

"There is no fear in love. But perfect love drives out fear." I John 4:18 NIV84

I visited Miss C. in an assisted-living community recently. She allowed me into her apartment but did so with an obvious frown on her face. She refused communion and shared with me that she had lost all confidence in a loving and caring God. As I tried to find some connection with Miss C., she only expressed more of her doubts and frustrations. I finally asked her what it would take for her to be convinced that God is ready to lavish her with His love. She said, "I've got to see Him come in here and tell me."

I smiled and told her, "He just did." Miss C. continued to frown.

With her permission I prayed that God would send someone else into her life this week to tell her about His love for her. As I left, I asked her what she was going to do when God sent another "love-bearing" visitor to her door. Miss C. smiled. So did I. And I think that God smiled too.

Some people are just afraid and need some TLC.

WEEK 44–THURSDAY

"When he came to his senses, he said, 'How many of my father's hired servants have food to spare, and here I am starving to death.'" Luke 15:17 NIRV

During my rebellious college years, I woke up one Easter morning with a hangover in an empty apartment. I remembered how much I enjoyed Easter Sunday in my past. Worship always seemed more exciting to me and the family dinners only added to the joy of the day. As I sat alone reflecting on some of my bad choices (with no food or money), I became very aware of my resurrected Lord.

I came to my senses and longed to be back in my Father's house. Life was so much better there. In my needy state, I began to remember the seeds of God's love that were planted in my heart and turned to Him in prayer (it had been a while). I cried as I asked for His forgiveness, and cried even more when I experienced it.

In my pathetic state, I experienced Easter in a new and exciting way.

WEEK 44–FRIDAY

"I now realize how true it is that God does not show favoritism but accepts from every nation the one who fear him and does what is right." Acts 10:34–35 NIRV

The Apostle Peter was guilty of showing favoritism, which means he was promoting the interests of Jewish people while neglecting the interests of the Gentiles. Even though Peter was a great leader in the Church, he had some issues that God had to change regarding showing favoritism in ministry. It took three visions from God, Gentiles knocking on his door, and recognizing his own prejudice in order for him to cross that Gentile barrier and accept them as fellow believers. God was about to do a new thing but Peter wanted to hold on to the old.

This was a defining moment in the early years of the Church.

Peter changed. So can we. God does not show favoritism but accepts men from every nation and nationality. It is easy to greet people from other cultures when they visit your congregation. They do that at Walmart. It is something else to cross some barriers and accept them as brothers and sisters.

Are you guilty of showing favoritism?

Catching the Moments

What moments stand out to you from this past week?

What verse of Scripture was important to you during the past week?

In seven words or fewer, describe this past week.

_____

_____

_____

_____

_____

_____

_____

_____

WEEK 45–SUNDAY

"Surrender yourself to the Lord, and wait patiently for him."
Psalm 37:7 GW

My dad graduated from Concordia Seminary in Springfield, Illinois, in 1944. As he awaited his first call to a congregation, he told the Lord, "I will go anywhere you want . . . except New York City." For those who don't know, Dad spent twenty-three years of his ministry in southeast Queens of New York City. As my dad told me this story years later, he said to me, "Never say *never* to the Lord."

Even though I loved the Lord dearly, I used to say, "I will never be a pastor!" When I was twenty-nine years old, that all changed. Somehow it seems that our "nevers" often become the very thing God calls us to do!

I love that old hymn "I Surrender All": "All to Jesus, I surrender; All to Him I freely give!" When we truly learn to surrender all, even our "nevers" bring joy into our lives. Some see surrender as a sign of weakness. That may be true, but it's in my weakness that I discover God's strength.

Never say never!

WEEK 45–MONDAY

"When Moses' hands grew tired, they took a stone and put it under him and he sat on it. Aaron and Hur held his hands up—one on one side, one on the other—so that his hands remained steady till sunset." Exodus 17:12 NIV84

The Amalekites had just attacked the Israelites and the Israelites fought against them at Rephidim. Moses stood on top of the hill overlooking the battle with the staff of God raised in his hands. As long as he held up his hands, God's people were winning, and whenever he lowered his hands, the Amalekites were winning.

Aaron and Hur noticed that Moses's hands were growing tired and came to his assistance. Each of them helped Moses lift up his hands, and victory came to God's people.

We all face spiritual battles as followers of Jesus. One of the keys in being victorious is symbolically keeping our hands lifted to the Lord, but sometimes we just get tired and weary. Thank God for those people who support us and help us keep our hands steady.

Pay attention to those around you who are finding it hard to keep their hands lifted.

WEEK 45–TUESDAY

> *"When the Counselor comes, whom I will send to you from the Father, the Spirit of truth who goes out from the Father, he will testify about me." John 15:26 NIV84*

The third article of the Apostle's Creed begins with "I believe in the Holy Spirit." He is the Third Person of the Holy Trinity. He is not a force or an idea but God Himself. He just didn't just show up in the New Testament. He is God and was there in the beginning. Without Him there would be no conviction of our sins and we would be unable to understand Scripture or receive spiritual guidance from our Heavenly Father. Technically, He is the One who lives in the hearts of believers, while Christ sits at the right hand of the Father—awaiting the day when He returns for the second time.

The Holy Spirit is mentioned fifty-nine times in the Book of Acts, and on thirty-six occasions, He is speaking or giving guidance to the followers of Jesus.

I believe in the Holy Spirit. He testifies to me about Jesus.

> *"However, do not rejoice that the spirits submit to you, but rejoice that your names are written in heaven." Luke 10:20 NIV84*

Jesus had sent out seventy-two disciples to preach repentance, lay hands on the sick, and cast out demons in His name. These disciples returned with excitement and said with joy, "Lord, even the demons submit to us in your name." Wow! They had to be pumped up as they experienced the power of God flow through their lives. Jesus had given them authority to overcome all the power of the enemy. *However,* Jesus did not want them to rejoice that spirits submit to them (because they were really submitting to Him). He wanted them to rejoice that their names were written in heaven.

How do you get your name written in heaven? It's not by attending a membership class or casting out demons. It's by repenting of your sins and believing in Jesus Christ as your personal Lord and Savior. When you humbly come before Him in faith, He writes your name in His book.

I truly rejoice when I think that "Steve Roth" is written down in heaven.

> *"On that day Gad went to David and said to him, 'Go up and build an altar to the Lord on the threshing floor of Araunah the Jebusite.'" 2 Samuel 24:18 NIV84*

David was instructed to purchase the threshing floor of a man named Araunah and build an altar on it to offer his sacrifice. This piece of land had a rich history and an important future. 2 Chronicles 3:1 informs us that this same threshing floor was on Mount Moriah, which was the same hill that Abraham offered Isaac and also where Jesus would die on the cross. It would also be the site of where Solomon would build the temple.

Araunah wanted to give David this land, but David said, "No, I insist on paying you for it. I will not sacrifice to the Lord my God burnt offerings that cost me nothing" (24:24). If David had accepted this offer, it would have no longer been David's sacrifice but Araunah's.

Jesus said that there is a cost in following Him (Luke 14:28), but it's all worth it.

Are your sacrifices costing you anything?

WEEK 45—FRIDAY

"So Abram went to live near the great trees of Mamre at Hebron, where he pitched his tents. There he built an altar to the Lord." Genesis 13:18 NIRV

Abraham had come to the moment of decision in regards to where he was going to establish his home. It was time for him to separate from his nephew, Lot, so Abraham allowed Lot to choose first. Lot chose Sodom, and Abraham was content to go in the opposite direction toward Hebron. When he got there, he pitched his tents and built an altar to the Lord.

In our search for buying a house in Texas, I have learned something very important. God's joy and peace is not found in a particular house but is found in a house where we choose to build an altar.

Finding a house that you like is important, but don't make the house an altar. Pitch your tent and build an altar to the Lord. That is where the Lord chooses to manifest His joy and peace.

You've got to ask yourself: "What does it mean to build an altar to the Lord in your home?"

Catching the Moments

What moments stand out to you from this past week?

What verse of Scripture was important to you during the past week?

In seven words or fewer, describe this past week.

"Religion that God our Father accepts as pure and faultless is this: to look after orphans and widows in their distress and to keep oneself from being polluted by the world." James 1:27 NIV84

Alison and I have been tremendously blessed to support an orphan in India for the past several years. His name is Matthew (just like our son). He loves his school and the children's home where he lives, and occasionally we get a letter from him. So many fatherless children in India have lost all hope in the future, but our monthly support is helping a young boy grow into manhood.

It was life-changing when I visited India on a mission trip several years ago. I was humbled by the witness of poor and persecuted Christians, and seeing so many orphans roaming the streets made me think twice about the luxury that I live in every day.

In order for our faith to be authentic, we must reach out to those less fortunate than ourselves.

Remember the fatherless and remember those women who have lost their husbands.

"He was accompanied by Nicodemus, the man who earlier had visited Jesus at night." John 19:39 NIV84

Nicodemus was that man who had cautiously gone to visit Jesus at night and was the recipient of Jesus's powerful words: "You must be born again" (John 3:7). In the beginning this man was afraid to be seen with Jesus, but in the end he was willing to stand up and claim His dead body. I am always amazed at how Jesus can transform a person's life. I know some people like that.

People who were once afraid to come to church were now praying for others. People who once mocked Jesus were now praising Him openly. People (like me) who were once afraid to mention the name of Jesus were given a boldness to preach about Him. Jesus changes people who hang out with Him. Weak and wimpy people are given the power of the Holy Spirit who transforms them. I still have my moments, but something happens to us when we are born again.

When I get to heaven, I want to find Nicodemus and have lunch with him.

WEEK 46–TUESDAY

> *"The right word at the right time is like precious gold set in silver." Proverbs 25:11 CEV*

I usually find it fulfilling preaching at funerals—even when the services are held outside of a Church sanctuary. I believe that people are more prone to listen to the Good News because they are more vulnerable.

I had such a funeral recently. I was filling in for someone else and found myself in a setting where I knew no one. As I waited for the service, I asked the Lord for something that would connect with the distraught people sitting in the chairs. God proved Himself faithful once again, and a predominantly unchurched crowd was listening to one scripture verse that God brought alive.

When I was done, one man told me that I hit it out of the park (I knew what he meant). Another man said, "When you lay your head on the pillow tonight, you can be assured that God used you to speak His truth to a hurting family." I was *so* humbled.

God's word spoken at the right time is **so** *precious.*

"Here I am! I stand at the door and knock. If anyone hears my voice and opens the door, I will come in and eat with him, and he with me." Revelation 3:20 NIV84

It's possible that many of you have heard this verse before, but what some might not realize is that Jesus was speaking these words to the Church in Laodicea. It had become so lukewarm (v. 16) that Jesus was on the outside of it trying to get back in. They were still a functioning church who thought they were rich, but Jesus called them poor. Yet Jesus did not give up on them.

I don't know about you, but I find the whole concept of Jesus trying to get back into the Church very scary. Can you picture Jesus knocking at the door of your Church asking permission to come in?

If you find yourself "lukewarm," it is time to repent and ask Jesus to come back into the center of your life.

"He who has an ear, let him hear what the Spirit says to the churches" (v. 22).

"Samson led Israel for twenty years in the days of the Philistines." Judges 15:20 NIV84

This verse speaks to me about being faithful in what God has called us to do. In the midst of Samson's fascinating story line we are simply told that he was faithful to do what God called him for. We don't know the details of those twenty years, except that Samson was called to lead .. . and he led.

Moses's story line is equally as exciting, but we know little about his life during the forty years after fleeing from Pharaoh . . . except that he faithfully tended the flock of Jethro, his father-in-law. Zechariah and Elizabeth served the Lord faithfully and unnoticed for years before being blessed with their son, John the Baptist. Simeon faithfully served the Lord for his whole life, and then he got to see the Messiah. Anna fasted and prayed in the temple for many years before meeting the baby Jesus. Do you see where I am going?

Stay faithful in your prayers and service to the Lord.

Even if no one else seems to notice what you are doing, God does and He will reward it.

WEEK 46–FRIDAY

> *"The apostles left the Sanhedrin, rejoicing because they had been counted worthy of suffering disgrace for the Name." Acts 5:41 NIV84*

Life in full-time ministry has been trying at times, but I must be honest: I've had it pretty easy. I was raised in a loving Christian family and have a wonderful wife and two great children. I've never been persecuted because of my faith in Jesus. I've gotten paid a good salary to do what I love and had my housing and benefits provided for many years. In retirement I have a manageable income and am able to continue in ministry. Have I had some low moments? Absolutely! Have I had to suffer disgrace for the name of Jesus? No. Not compared to what others have had to endure. I've had some inconvenience . . . at worst.

I don't share all this because I have a desire to be persecuted. I share it because I realize how blessed I have been. God has been so good to my wife and me, and I never want to take my blessed life for granted.

Thank you, Lord, for filling my life with so many good things.

Catching the Moments

What moments stand out to you from this past week?

What verse of Scripture was important to you during the past week?

In seven words or fewer, describe this past week.

_____

_____

_____

_____

_____

_____

_____

_____

_____

_____

_____

_____

_____

WEEK 47–SUNDAY

"For every animal of the forest is mine, and the cattle on a thousand hills." Psalm 50:10 NIV84

My wife once purchased a framed picture at a yard sale. It's a winter scene with a few cattle grazing on the side of a hill. When I asked Alison why she bought it, she said it reminded her of her cow. You see, Alison loves how our God is portrayed as someone who owns the cattle on a thousand hills. Whenever we have been in need, she would say, "Lord, all I need is just one of your cows to meet my needs."

I've grown to love that picture because it reminds me that our God is able to provide all our needs. It now hangs over the desk in my office.

God is the divine owner of cattle on a thousand hills. Sometimes He has given a cow just when we need it, and other times He's given us a whole herd.

It's good to place some visuals around your home to remind you of God's goodness and His provision.

He will meet all your needs, and sometimes all it takes is a cow.

WEEK 47–MONDAY

"Then, knowing what lies ahead for you, you won't become bored with being a Christian nor become spiritually dull and indifferent, but you will be anxious to follow the example of those who receive all that God has promised them because of their strong faith and patience." Hebrews 6:12 TLB

"Maintenance ministry" is too prevalent in today's Church. If you don't know what that is, let me try to explain it in one sentence: taking care of a congregation in order to just keep it alive. It happens to the best of us, but long-term "maintenance mode" is not what Jesus intended for His Church. His command was to "Go, make disciples, grow, lead souls to salvation, and make a difference outside your walls."

Is your congregation in maintenance mode? If so, don't give up. There is time for a change. Get a few people together of kindred spirit, repent, and ask the Lord to give you a fresh vision for *His* Church. Follow the example of those who were devoted to ministry and not just maintenance.

Jesus will answer that prayer!

WEEK 47—TUESDAY

> *"I looked for a man among them who would build up the wall and stand before me in the gap on behalf of the land so I would not have to destroy it, but I found none." Ezekiel 22:30 NIV84*

God was looking for real godly men, those He could rely on to build up the wall around His people and stand in the gap on behalf of them . . . but He couldn't find one. How sad! God is still looking for men of God. Men, can He count on you?

Let me be blunt! We need more men to stand up and be counted within the Church—guys who are serious about taking on leadership roles in the Church and the home. It doesn't take any faith to put on a suit and sit in a pew on Sunday morning; a man of God is more concerned with *being* the Church than *going to* church. It doesn't take any faith to follow your girlfriend to church; a man of God brings her to church.

It doesn't take any faith to point out the gaps in his family; a man of God stands in those gaps.

WEEK 47—WEDNESDAY

"Therefore, since we have been justified through faith, we have peace with God through our Lord Jesus Christ."
Romans 5:1 NIV84

I can attest to the fact that the peace of God truly does transcend human understanding. It can keep us calm in the midst of turmoil and can guard our hearts and minds from anxiety. Money can't buy this incredible gift. But here's something to consider: we cannot experience the peace *of* God until we first have peace *with* God.

Jesus Christ is our peace (Eph. 2:14) and we are justified with God through faith in Him. In other words, we have peace with God through His death and resurrection. Once I have peace with God, I can now experience the peace of God.

God's peace comes from within. It enables our souls to remain at rest—even when external circumstances are all against us. Jesus told us that in this world we will have plenty of trouble, but we should not worry.

It's very important that I ask you: Are you at peace with God?

WEEK 47—THURSDAY

"Give thanks to the Lord." I Chronicles 16:8 NIV84

I thank God for the ability to take my dog for a walk.

I thank God for a wife whom I get to pray with, laugh with, and communicate with.

I thank God for shrimp scampi.

I thank God for the hope that takes me through my valleys.

I thank God for planting eternity in my heart.

I thank God for my recliner, where I get to relax and sleep.

I thank God for all those who have forgiven me over the years.

I thank God for giving me love and joy through my children.

I thank God for a Savior who loved me enough to die for me.

I thank God for the privilege of getting to preach and teach the Word of God.

I thank God for central air-conditioning during Texas summers.

I thank God for the times when the Holy Spirit has whispered in my ear, "Don't go there."

I thank God for Chik-fil-A.

I thank God for people who can give thanks without being "super-spiritual."

Happy Thanksgiving!

WEEK 47–FRIDAY

> *"Watch out! Be on your guard against all kinds of greed; life does not consist in an abundance of possessions." Luke 12:15 NIV84*

I love a good deal as much as the next guy, but Black Friday always reminds me of something that happened in 2008. As a national chain opened its doors at 5:00 a. m., an out-of-control mob trampled one worker to death and knocked over many others to the ground. Why? For 75 percent off! This happened about a mile from where we were living in Valley Stream. Every Black Friday I think back to that man who lost his life because of people who wanted to grab up those TVs on sale. I'm guessing that some of those shoppers were great people who just got caught up in the moment.

Greed is a selfish and excessive desire for more of something than is needed. It can change the way you act and make you do things you thought you'd never do. It's not wrong to take advantage of today's deals. Just remember Jesus's words: "Watch out! Be on your guard against all kinds of greed."

Be a light on Black Friday!

WEEK 47–SATURDAY

Catching the Moments

What moments stand out to you from this past week?

What verse of Scripture was important to you during the past week?

In seven words or fewer, describe this past week.

_____

_____

_____

_____

_____

_____

"Prepare the way for the Lord." Matthew 3:3 NIV84

Advent is a season of four Sundays before Christmas when we prepare ourselves for the celebration of Christ's birth. Advent comes from two Latin words: *ad-venire*, which means "to come to." Although this season is not found in the Bible, its meaning is found throughout Scripture.

Just as John the Baptist prepared the way for the Messiah, it is good for us to prepare ourselves for a fresh encounter with our Messiah, Jesus Christ. We spend a lot of time (and money) preparing our homes for the day of Christmas, but how much time do we spend preparing our hearts for Jesus to come to us in new and exciting ways? I want more than additional head knowledge about Jesus. I want to personally experience Him at work in my life. I want Advent to be more than a religious ritual when I merely light another candle each week. I want His kingdom to come and His will to be done . . . *right here and right now.*

If you share the same desire, prepare yourself for the Lord to "rock" your world.

WEEK 48–MONDAY

"You are without excuse, every one of you who passes judgment. For by the standard by which you judge another you condemn yourself, since you, the judge, do the very same things." Romans 2:1 NAB

We all have our pet peeves—those annoying little things that can "push our buttons." Some of my pet peeves are as follows:

· People who don't know how to park their car next to a parking meter.

- People who finish your sentence.

- Chain messages that you must share on Facebook with five of your friends if you want God to bless you.

- People who use five hundred words to describe something that could be described easily in fifty words.

- Parents who tell their disobedient child "one more time" ten times.

- People who misinterpret spiritual *passion* for a lack of conformity.

- People who think that God approves of their denomination above all others.

- Churches that take five offerings—in one service.

I'm learning something in my senior years: some of my habits are other people's pet peeves.

Lord, help me not to pass judgment on someone else based on my pet peeves.

WEEK 48–TUESDAY

> *"So I find this law at work: Although I want to do good, evil is right there with me." Romans 7:21 NIRV*

There is an old Cherokee story about a grandfather teaching his grandson about the battle taking place within him between good and evil. This wise old man said that the conflict is like a fight between two wolves. One wolf is evil and the other wolf is good. After thinking about his illustration, the grandson asked him, "So which wolf will win, Grandfather?" The wise old Native American replied, "The one you feed."

Jesus Christ came to give us a new and renewed nature. This new man who now lives within us is empowered by the Holy Spirit and guides us into all life and truth. But that old, sinful man always tries to find his way back into our lives. While Christ has already won the victory over sin, death, and the devil, it is good to ask ourselves occasionally: Which nature are we feeding? The old sinful nature or the new one we receive by faith?

"Thanks be to God, who delivers me through Jesus Christ our Lord." (Romans 7:25)

WEEK 48–WEDNESDAY

"Your love continues forever; your loyalty goes on and on like the sky." Psalm 89:2 (NCV)

I've got to admit, there are some days when I'm just not feeling it. The things that I had been hoping for didn't happen. Sometimes my emotions get the better of me and I go into my solitary box and escape with whatever is on TV. I'm sure you've had those days when you don't feel like praying or reading the Word. My love for the Lord is still there, but it gets buried beneath my burden of self-pity. I know things will get better, but for now, just leave me alone and let me sulk.

Let me tell you something absolutely incredible: God's love for me remains steadfast and His loyalty toward me goes on and on. The love that Jesus showed for me when He went to the cross continues toward me—even when I sulk. He remains faithful and loyal toward me even when I am faithless toward Him. It just goes on and on and on and on . . .

Thank You, Lord, that even when I lose my witness, I never lose my Savior.

"He saw the disciples straining at the oars." Mark 6:48 NIV84

After Jesus had fed the five thousand, He made His disciples get into a boat and go ahead of Him to Bethsaida. Later that night, while He was up on a mountaintop praying, Jesus saw His disciples straining at the oars. He had purposely sent His disciples on a boat ride into a storm, and even though it was dark and they seemingly were out of sight, *He saw them straining.* And here is the Good News: He came to them and calmed the storm.

Sometimes ministry and life can be very difficult. In fact, there have been many scary moments when I've found myself straining to move forward in the midst of stormy times. Here is the Good News: my Savior always sees my straining and always shows up.

He climbs into my boat, seems to look straight into my heart, and says, "Steve, stop straining. It's Me. You don't have to be afraid." Calm comes, hope is restored, and to this day . . . it still amazes me.

Don't give up, my friend. God knows what is going on.

WEEK 48-FRIDAY

"Enter through the narrow gate. For wide is the gate and broad is the road that leads to destruction, and many enter it. But small is the gate and narrow the road that leads to life, and only a few find it." Matthew 7:13–14 NIV84

The gate to our salvation is a very narrow gate. While it is open to anyone, only a few find it. Jesus also said in Matthew 22:14, "For many are invited, but few are chosen." This leads me to ask the question, "Lord, are only a few people going to be saved?" (Luke 13:23)

While we do not know the number of people who will be saved, we do know it will be *few*. Jesus said so. It's safe to say that fewer than half of all people will be saved. What else could "few" refer to?

There are not many gates into heaven. Only one, and His name is Jesus. Someone once asked me why I was so narrow-minded when talking about heaven. My response was simple: it's a narrow gate.

Get off the road that leads to destruction. God's grace has made a way!

WEEK 48–SATURDAY

Catching the Moments

What moments stand out to you from this past week?

What verse of Scripture was important to you during the past week?

In seven words or fewer, describe this past week.

_____

_____

_____

_____

_____

_____

_____

_____

_____

> *"God intends something gloriously grand here and is making the decisions that will bring it about." John 8:50 MSG*

Christ's humility is obvious here as He talks about His Father in heaven. I love how *The Message* portrays the function of His Father.

I can't help but think that my heavenly Father is working the same way in my life. He intends to do something gloriously grand in my life and is also making the decisions that will bring it about. He is able to see the whole picture, not just the circumstances I find myself in. People may oppose me, mock me, curse me, and belittle me, but my daddy has something gloriously grand planned for my life. That's who our Heavenly Father is: Someone who is working all things together for our good (Rom. 8:28). Do you believe that? Don't let others misinterpret who God is. His love for you is so incredible. It goes beyond what you could ask or even imagine.

If you find yourself in a difficult situation, why not repeat the preceding verse with some faith and confidence?

WEEK 49—MONDAY

> *"Therefore, I am all the more eager to send him, so that when you see him again you may be glad and I may have less anxiety." Philippians 2:28 NIV84*

Paul was informing the Philippian Church that he was sending his coworker and fellow soldier (2:25) Epaphroditus to visit them. Paul couldn't come because he was in prison, so he knew they would be encouraged by his friend's visit and he would have "less anxiety."

Now I know that we are not to be anxious about anything (see 4:6), but Paul still had his moments of anxiety in caring for the sheep under his care. I get that! Paul didn't worry about his own needs, but when it came to the souls of others, he still occasionally worried.

After spending thirty-two years shepherding the same flock, I still worry about some of them. It's like your own children—even though we are not supposed to worry, we still do. But here's the thing—when I entrust them into the care of the Great Shepherd, I have "less anxiety."

Be an Epaphroditus to someone else.

WEEK 49–TUESDAY

"And they spread among the Israelites a bad report about the land they had explored." Numbers 13:32 NIV84

Here's a bit of Bible trivia you can pass along to someone else. Who are these people: Shammua, Shaphat, Igal, Palti, Gaddiel, Gaddi, Ammiel, Sethur, Nahbit, and Geuel? Since you have already read the preceding verse, you can probably guess. They are ten of the twelve spies who were chosen to explore the Promised Land (13:4–16). They were the ones who spread a bad report among the two million Israelites.

The other two spies you would recognize: Joshua and Caleb. They saw the same giants that the other ten saw, but they clung to the promise of God that the Promised Land belonged to them. Caleb said, "We should go up and take possession of the land, for we can certainly do it" (13:30).

Whose report will you believe? Those who spread a bad report full of doubt and unbelief will not likely be remembered in the long run. But those who spread Good News are usually remembered.

The majority is not always right.

WEEK 49—WEDNESDAY

"Such confidence as this is ours through Christ before God. Not that we are competent in ourselves, but our competence comes from God. He has made us competent as ministers of a new covenant." 2 Corinthians 3:4–6 NIV84

I recently came across my report card from fourth grade. I had to smile as I read Mrs. Hersey's (my teacher) comments after each marking period: *(1st) Steven is a good steady pupil. He does lack self-confidence. (2nd) Steven is a conscientious pupil. He adds a great deal to our class discussions and class projects. (3rd) Steven has contributed much to our art work in our unit. He is well-liked by his classmates but still lack self-confidence. (4th) Steven needs to contribute more to the <u>entire</u> class. He is very self-reserved!* (The underline and exclamation point are Mrs. Hersey's.)

Hmmm. I'm still like that at times, yet God called me into the ministry. Go figure! I still lack confidence in myself, but I have plenty in Jesus. I can still be very self-reserved and don't always contribute to the *entire* class but have been very blessed to be loved by most of my classmates.

God doesn't call the qualified; He qualifies the called.

WEEK 49—THURSDAY

"If you love me, show it by doing what I've told you. I will talk to the Father, and he'll provide you another Friend so that you will always have someone with you. This Friend is the Spirit of Truth." John 14:15–17 MSG

I have a Friend who is always there for me. He explains things to me about Jesus, He reminds me of things I need to know, and He always guides me in the right direction. This Friend is the Holy Spirit. Why is it that so many people have portrayed the Third Person of the Holy Trinity as this scary ghost who turns you into a crazy fanatic?

Six times in the Gospel of John, chapters 14, 15, and 16, Eugene Peterson, author of *The Message*, refers to the Holy Spirit as "Friend" (with a capital *F*). I love it!

He's not a "slap me five" type of Friend but the One who makes my relationship with God very personal. He's a Friend who wants nothing but the highest good for me.

Why not surrender your life to His Friendship? It will change your life!

WEEK 49–FRIDAY

> *"But God chose the foolish things of the world to shame the wise; God chose the weak things of the world to shame the strong." I Corinthians 1:27 NIV84*

Sometimes I really believe God has given me the "Gift of Foolishness." For example, there have been times when I am in the company of some colleagues (far more educated than myself) and I will come out with something not found in any textbook. I'm not talking about something theologically deep; I'm talking about something practically foolish. I'm convinced that the Lord Jesus gave me this precious gift to burst a few bubbles. Don't get me wrong! I stand in awe of those who are able to use their intellect to the glory of God. They amaze me! But the same Holy Spirit who works through their education is able to work through my foolishness.

When God chose the foolish things of the world, I was near the front of the line. Each of us is an important tool in God's tool box. Don't minimize your importance.

He specializes in choosing the foolish, weak, and lowly.

Catching the Moments

What moments stand out to you from this past week?

What verse of Scripture was important to you during the past week?

In seven words or fewer, describe this past week.

_____

_____

_____

_____

_____

_____

_____

_____

_____

_____

_____

_____

> *"Where, O death, is your victory? Where, O death, is your sting?" I Corinthians 15:55 NIV84*

Even though the melody to the great hymn "Abide with Me" is on the somber side, I firmly believe it should be sung with confidence. I especially like the last two verses.

I fear no foe with Thee at hand to bless;
Ills have no weight and tears no bitterness.
Where is death's sting? Where, grave, thy victory?
I triumph still is Thou abide with me!

When I am about to leave this world, I pray that God's grace would enable me to have this same attitude: No fear! No guilt! No bitterness! The sting of death has no hold on me, because *Jesus abides with me.* All of us will face death some day, but because of Jesus, we will triumph over it. When that moment comes, I want my prayer to be:

Hold Thou Thy cross before my closing eyes,
Shine through the gloom, and point me to the skies.
Heav'ns morning breaks and earth's vain shadows flee;
In life, in death, O Lord, abide with me.

I triumph still if Thou abide with me.

> *"If you do away with the yoke of oppression, with the pointing of the finger and malicious talk . . . then your light will rise in the darkness, and your night will become like the noonday." Isaiah 58:9–10 NIV84*

I don't know about you, but I'm still too familiar with the pointing of my finger. I still have moments when I'd rather point the finger at someone else's fault rather than dealing with my own.

Do you know where "finger-pointing" began? In the Garden of Eden! When God confronted Adam with his sin, he pointed the finger at Eve. He blamed "the woman you put here with me" (Gen. 3:12). When Eve was confronted with her sin, she said, "The devil made me do it" (Gen. 3:13). Sin makes us all very self-righteous.

After all these years, I'm starting to learn something very important: When I take responsibility for my own sin and stop pointing the finger at others, God's light rises in my darkness and restores my joy and purpose. I'm learning not to blame others (and the devil) for the sins that I am guilty of.

Don't judge someone just because they sin differently than you.

WEEK 50—TUESDAY

> ***One day Jesus was praying in a certain place. When he finished, one of his disciples said to him, "Lord, teach us to pray, just as John taught his disciples." Luke 11:1 NIV84***

Whenever I read this verse, I picture the disciples watching Jesus while He was in prayer. They obviously saw something in Jesus's prayer life that they wanted. When He was finished, one of them asked him to teach them how to pray. They had now been following Jesus for a couple years and were used to watching Him pray to His Father. I love Jesus's response: "When you pray . . ." Not *if* you pray, *when* you pray. In other words, just do it. Then He gave them a prayer that they could use as a model—we call it the Lord's Prayer.

When I find myself mindlessly mouthing the words of the Lord's Prayer, I still ask the Lord to teach me how to pray. You see, sometimes my prayer life can become very dry and ritualistic. God, forgive me! It's then I usually say, "Lord, teach me how to pray with honesty and power."

What was the last thing God taught you about prayer?

WEEK 50–WEDNESDAY

> *"Ezra praised the LORD, the great God; and all the people lifted their hands and responded, 'Amen! Amen!'"*
> *Nehemiah 8:6 NIV84*

The story is told of a Christian man who lived in the countryside of England at the beginning of the twentieth century. A business opportunity enabled him to travel to London for the first time in his life. After he had finished his business, he made plans to visit two large churches he had heard a lot about. The preachers at both congregations were well-known around the world and attracted quite a crowd each week. When the businessman returned home, his wife inquired about his visit to both places. The man explained how both places were exciting to visit but he appreciated the second one over the first. At the first church, people talked openly about the great preacher they had; at the second one, they talked about the great God they served.

The best preaching should leave people talking more about the message than the messenger. While it is not wrong to thank the messenger, a good sermon should always leave the people praising the greatness of God. Amen! Amen!

Thank God for the message!

WEEK 50–THURSDAY

> *"Now the Berean Jews were of more noble character than those in Thessalonica, for they received the message with great*

eagerness and examined the Scriptures every day to see if what Paul said was true." Acts 17:11 NIRV

I think I would have loved hanging out with the Bereans. They were people who hungered for the Word of God, and when Paul preached, they received with open hearts. But it didn't stop there. When they got home, they studied the Scriptures for themselves to see is what Paul preached was true.

There are those who listen to the Word, and then there are those who study the Word. We must become people who study the Word on a daily basis. If you make it a habit, your faith will blossom. How do we study the Word? You can start by having a concordance and a reliable commentary. Having another version of Scripture is also helpful. Ask someone you trust to give some study methods that will help you examine the Word. (Relying upon the Holy Spirit is always helpful too.)

Believers listen to the Word. Disciples study the Word.

WEEK 50—FRIDAY

"But our citizenship is in heaven. And we eagerly await a Savior from there, the Lord Jesus Christ." Philippians 3:20 NIV84

Our home address book is one that we printed out years ago. It's a mess, but it works for us. Throughout the years, we never took the time update it; we'd just cross out an address and write in the new one. You can imagine what our book looks like. Recently, I was looking up an address and came across the name of a close friend who had died and gone to be with the Lord. Alison had crossed out her address and inserted her new address as *heaven*. It brought a smile to my face.

This world is not our permanent address. As believers in Jesus, God has a new address awaiting all of us. Our citizenship and our home are in heaven. I wonder if God's Book of Life has an address printed next to my name?

While I'm not looking to die, I do eagerly await the day when my Savior will submit a permanent change-of-address form for me.

"I'm but a stranger here, Heav'n is my home."

Catching the Moments

What moments stand out to you from this past week?

What verse of Scripture was important to you during the past week?

In seven words or fewer, describe this past week.

_____

_____

_____

_____

_____

_____

_____

_____

_____

_____

> *"Carry each other's burdens, and in this way you will fulfill the law of Christ." Galatians 6:2 NIV84*

To carry someone else's burdens is to sympathize with and become involved in their life so they do not have to face their trials and burdens alone. When we help others carry their burden, we are being obedient to Christ's command. Because Jesus carried all of our burdens, He will give us the strength we need to help other people carry theirs.

There is that phase repeated so many times: "People don't care how much you know until they know how much you care." You don't need a degree or more theological training in order to help someone who is burdened. The love of Christ has been shown to you so that you can show it to others.

Don't be quick to criticize others who may be under a tremendous burden. Show them how much you care. Don't evaluate their burden; carry it. Don't pity them; fulfill the law of Christ's love by helping them carry their load.

Thank You, Lord, for carrying my burdens. Help me to carry others.

WEEK 51—MONDAY

> *"I will lead the blind by ways they have not known, along unfamiliar paths I will guide them; I will turn the darkness into light before them and make the rough places smooth." Isaiah 42:16 NIV84*

We all want God to lead us and guide us. Sometimes He leads us along familiar paths, and then there are those times when He leads us along those unfamiliar ones.

I am a guy! I like to be in control when I'm driving to a location where I have the route planned out. But when God's destination is unknown, even my GPS is not helpful. When we moved to Texas, our GPS occasionally gave us confused directions because a few roads were so new that my GPS was unable to calculate our route.

We can trust the Lord's guidance, especially when we are traveling unfamiliar paths. God is so trustworthy that even when a path does not exist, He'll create one! Don't be afraid of unfamiliar paths. They lead to some incredible places.

Is it time to recalculate?

WEEK 51—TUESDAY

"Suddenly a great company of the heavenly host appeared with the angel." Luke 2:13 NIV84

Angels are such an important part of the Christmas story, but let's make sure we get our facts straight about them. They are immortal spirits created by God. Demons and Satan are fallen angels. There are two angels for every demon. We do not become angels when we die. Jesus was not and is not an angel; He is God and created them. Angels are not allowed to be worshipped; only God is. Angels can manifest themselves in human form. Our English word "angel" comes from the Greek *angelos*, which means "messenger."

What are their functions? Angels are messengers (Luke 2:11 and Luke 24:5–8). Angels are sent to serve (Hebrews 1:14 and Luke 22:43). Angels guard and protect us (Ps. 91:11 and Ps. 34:7). Angels war/fight against evil spirits (Rev. 12:7 and Dan. 10:13). Angels worship God (Luke 2:13–14 and Isa. 6:1–4).

Pay close attention to strangers this Christmas season, because "some people have entertained angels without knowing it." Hebrews 13:2

> *"Glory to God in the highest, and on earth peace to men on whom his favor rests." Luke 2:14 NIV84*

This time of year, we see and hear the word "peace" everywhere we go. It makes me wonder, if Jesus came to bring peace, why is our nation so divided? Why are Christians divided so strongly on denominational lines? Why is the tension in race relations getting worse? Why are families more divided now than ever before? Where is the peace announced by the angels?

Let me share some scriptures that might help.

- Before we can have the peace *of* God, we must have peace *with* God—Romans 5:1.

- God's peace is different than the world's peace. It's not an absence of trouble or pain but an inner confidence that He is always with us—John 14:27.

- God's peace is perfect—Isaiah 26:3.

- God's peace goes beyond our human understanding—Philippians 4:7.

- God's peace is found in a person—Ephesians 2:14.

Real peace is not found in a philosophy, a religion, or the right denomination. It is found in the person of Jesus Christ.

> *"Be still and know that I am God." Psalm 46:10 NIV84*

"O little town of Bethlehem, how still we see thee lie."

"Silent Night, Holy Night, all is calm, all is bright."

"Away in a manger, no crib for a bed, The little Lord Jesus laid down his sweet head."

We sing about stillness at Christmas but don't always experience it. What is stillness?

- A place where we cease striving, relax, let go, and let God be God

- A place of serenity and tranquility

- A place where we can appreciate the wonder of God in the face of a baby

- A place where you are so quiet in your spirit that you can hear God speak

- A place where you appreciate the presence of God in the little things

I pray that we can rediscover the power of stillness. Don't let the trappings of Christmas distract you from this heavenly place of fellowship. Rediscover the wonder and awesomeness of Christ's birth. He is an incredible God—filled with wonder, awe, power, amazement, mystery, miracles, peace, joy, excitement, love, hope, victory, restoration, deliverance, and forgiveness.

God's plea to each of us is "Be still and know that I am God."

WEEK 51 -FRIDAY

"She . . . placed him in a manger." Luke 2:7 NIV84

I find this verse absolutely amazing. Mary took God Incarnate and placed Him in a feeding trough of smelly animals in a dirty stable.

It may not have been all that appealing, but it was where the Father wanted Jesus to be. It wasn't a permanent place but had its purpose. Mary and Joseph didn't complain that their son had to be born in a barn; they treasured the moment.

Jesus would later be placed upon the cross, and now He is placed at the right hand of the Father—preparing a place for us. It only gets better with Jesus!

Did you know that your Father has placed you right where He wants you to be? Your manger may not be all that appealing, but God's purpose for you is where He has placed you. Don't complain about your placement; treasure the moment! As you get ready to celebrate Christmas, take a moment to thank the Lord for placing Jesus in your life . . . and also thank Him for your manger. It has its purpose!

Merry Christmas!

WEEK 51–SATURDAY

Catching the Moments

What moments stand out to you from this past week?

What verse of Scripture was important to you during the past week?

In seven words or fewer, describe this past week.

_____

_____

_____

_____

"You are my mighty rock, my fortress, my protector, the rock where I am safe, my shield, my powerful weapon, and my place of shelter." Psalm 18:2 CEV

David sang to the Lord the words of this psalm after He had delivered him from his enemies. Can you imagine David boldly declaring his praises to God with the following words? Lord, You are . . .

- my Mighty Rock—You are my unmovable foundation.

- my Protector—You are my Bodyguard.

- my Rock where I'm safe—You are a granite hideout.

- my Shield—You are my Protection against Satan's arrows.

- my Powerful Weapon—You fight my battles.

- my Place of Shelter—You make me feel safe and confident.

What a powerful confession of faith! God, forgive me for those times when You've given me victory and deliverance and I've forgotten to praise You. If He has just brought you a victory, why not set aside some time to boldly open your mouth and thank Him.

In your time alone with the Lord, finish this sentence: Lord, You are _____.

"Who is a God like you, who pardons sin and forgives the transgression of the remnant of his inheritance? You do not stay angry forever but delight to show mercy." Micah 7:18 NIV84

Don't reject the pardon that God offers you.

In 1833 there was an interesting case brought before the Supreme Court, *US v. Wilson*, that addressed the issue of pardon. George Wilson had been found guilty of robbing the U. S. Mail in Pennsylvania and sentenced to death. President Andrew Jackson would eventually offer a pardon, but Wilson refused to accept it.

Chief Justice Marshall eventually rendered the following decision on behalf of the Supreme Court: "Unless the recipient of the pardon accepts the pardon, then the pardon cannot be applied."

Our gracious and compassionate God sent His Son, Jesus Christ, to the cross so that our sins could be pardoned. Even though we are all guilty, all we have to do is accept His pardon by faith. Unless the recipient of the pardon accepts the pardon, then the pardon cannot be applied.

Who is a God like You? I accept Your pardon.

WEEK 52–TUESDAY

"We live by faith, not by sight." 2 Corinthians 5:7 NIV84

Years ago there was a short season in my life when I was virtually void of emotions. It was a very confusing time. For a couple months, I experienced no real joyful highs or sorrowful lows. Preaching became an act of faith, and carrying out my duties as a pastor was done simply out of obedience. I began to think something was wrong with me: *Lord, what is going on in my life?* God seemed to be quiet, but I remained faithful—as best I could.

Eventually my emotions began to be restored to normal and my emotional void was forgotten. One week, when my emotions were in high gear, the Lord reminded me about my confusing season I had just passed through: "I allowed you to go through that period to teach you an important lesson: walk by faith, not by how you feel. Well done!"

So much of what we do is based on our feelings, but what happens when those feelings do not respond to God's call on our life?

Holy Spirit, help me to walk by faith.

WEEK 52–WEDNESDAY

> *"As for other matters, brothers and sisters, we instructed you how to live in order to please God, as in fact you are living. Now we ask you and urge you in the Lord Jesus to do this more and more." I Thessalonians 4:1 NIRV*

Paul was commending the Thessalonians for lives that are pleasing to God. I love how he encouraged them to keep doing this "more and more." In verse 10 of this same chapter, he commends them for how they loved one another. Once again he tells them to keep doing so "more and more."

As we move into a new year, let me be the first to commend you on living a life that is pleasing to God and how you have shown the love of Jesus to others. Keep doing this "more and more."

It is easy to point out our flaws, but, at the same time, we need to be encouraged to keep doing what we are doing right. If our goal for next year is to live our lives to please the Lord and love one another, it will be a successful one.

Keep doing it "more and more."

WEEK 52–THURSDAY

> *"See, the Sovereign Lord comes with power, and he rules with a mighty arm. See, his reward is with him, and his recompense accompanies him. He tends his flock like a shepherd: He gathers the lambs in his arms and carries them close*

to his heart; he gently leads those that have young." Isaiah 40:10–11 NIRV

Our awesome God has two arms. One arm is mighty and powerful, and with it He rules the world. The other arm is tender as He shows compassion to the weak and wounded. God's awesomeness is seen in both His arms. If all we witnessed was His ruling arm, we would always be afraid of Him. If all we saw was His compassionate arm, the meaning of grace would be cheapened.

My God has two arms, and I have experienced both. He still makes my knees shake, but He also makes me want to run into His arms like a little kid.

If I had to describe my God to someone who doesn't know Him, I would probably start by describing His arms.

I long to be so close to the Lord that I can feel His heartbeat.

WEEK 52–FRIDAY

"As the men were leaving Jesus, Peter said to him, 'Master, it is good for us to be here. Let us put up three shelters—one for you, one for Moses and one for Elijah.'" Luke 9:33 NIV84

Jesus brought Peter, James, and John with him to the top of a mountain, and there something incredible happened. Jesus was transfigured from the inside out and the disciples "saw his glory," and He talked with Moses and Elijah. Peter was so awestruck that he wanted to build some shelters and stay put right there in that glorious moment. Mountaintop experiences are like that.

Jesus occasionally gives us those special glory moments—when He gives us a glimpse of His glory. Maybe it occurs on a retreat or during an anointed worship service or just a special moment alone with the Lord. We all know that we don't live our lives on top of mountaintop experiences, but they have their purpose. The memory of those glory moments helps us persevere in our walks through the valleys.

The same God who was with you on the mountain walks with you in the valley.

Catching the Moments

What moments stand out to you from this past week?

What verse of Scripture was important to you during the past week?

In seven words or fewer, describe this past week.

_____

_____

_____

_____

_____

_____

_____

_____

_____

_____

"Keep your eyes on Jesus, who both began and finished this race we're in. Study how he did it. Because he never lost sight of where he was headed—that exhilarating finish in and with God—he could put up with anything along the way: Cross, shame, whatever. And now he's there, in the place of honor, right alongside God. When you find yourselves flagging in your faith, go over that story again, item by item, that long litany of hostility he plowed through. That will shoot adrenaline into your souls!" Hebrews 12:2–3 MSG

Heavenly Father, when I become overwhelmed by my personal struggles, help me to remember all that Jesus went through. He was willing to endure the cross because of the joy He knew would be His afterward. I need that kind of endurance. Whenever my faith begins to waver, take me back again to what Jesus plowed through. Don't ever let me forget His story. Help me when I lose heart and grow weary, knowing that You are leading me to a place of joy. In Jesus's name. Amen.

Happy New Year! Catch the Moments!

Scripture Index

Job 42:7–W5–Tue

Psalm 1:2–W40–Mon

Psalm 13:3–W2–Wed

Psalm 16:11–W15–Wed

Psalm 18:2–W52–Sun

Psalm 19:14–W1–Mon

Psalm 23:4–W20–Tue

Psalm 30:5–W20–Wed

Psalm 30:7–W3–Sun

Psalm 33:22–W38–Sun

Psalm 37:3–W38–Tue

Psalm 37:4–W40–Tue

Psalm 37:7–W45–Sun

Psalm 37:23–W14–Wed

Psalm 40:1–W8–Thu

Psalm 40:3–W6–Sun

Psalm 42:2–W41–Thu

Psalm 46:1–W36–Fri

Psalm 46:10–W51–Thu

Psalm 50:10–W47–Sun

Psalm 51:12–W29–Thu

Psalm 51:17–W17–Fri

Psalm 84:6–W13–Tue

Psalm 85:2–W29–Tue

Psalm 89:2–W48–Wed

Psalm 90:8–W15–Tue

Psalm 91:1–W18–Tue

Psalm 91:11–W7–Thu

Psalm 95:2–W16–Fri

Psalm 107:2–W14–Fri

Psalm 111:10–W23–Wed

Psalm 116:15–W43–Fri

Psalm 118:24–W1–Sun

Psalm 119:10–W22–Fri

Psalm 139:14–W32–Thu

Psalm 147:3–W33–Mon

Psalm 147:18–W31–Sun

Psalm 148:3–W29–Fri

Proverbs 1:8–W19–Sun

Proverbs 6:16–W19–Wed

Proverbs 14:4–W31–Thu

Proverbs 14:15–W43–Thu

Proverbs 14:23–W36–Mon

Proverbs 15:14–W24–Thu

Proverbs 15:17–W32–Fri

Proverbs 18:8–W28–Tue

Proverbs 18:22–W35–Tue

Proverbs 22:6–W42–Mon

Proverbs 25:11–W46–Tue

Proverbs 27:23–W38–Thu

Proverbs 28:23–W42–Fri

Proverbs 31:8-9–W10–Wed

Ecclesiastes 3:1,4–W22–Tue

Ecclesiastes 10:10–W9–Tue

Isaiah 1:19–W16–Mon

Isaiah 30:21–W33–Sun

Isaiah 40:10-11–W52–Thu

Isaiah 40:12–W27–Mon

Isaiah 40:31–W6–Tue

Isaiah 42:16–W51–Mon

Isaiah 44:3–W3–Mon

Isaiah 46:4–W23–Tue

Isaiah 56:7–W3–Wed

Isaiah 58:9-10–W50–Mon

Isaiah 62:5–W41–Wed

Jeremiah 15:16–W16–Thu

Lamentations 3:20-23–
   W26–Mon

Ezekiel 16:49-50–W26–Fri

Ezekiel 22:30–W47–Tue

Ezekiel 36:26–W4–Thu

Ezekiel 46:9–W2–Thu

Ezekiel 47:1–W17–Thu

Ezekiel 47:9–W34–Wed

Daniel 1:17–W34–Mon

Daniel 2:20-21–W44–Mon

Daniel 3:25–W8–Mon

Daniel 6:22–W22–Wed

Hosea 13:6–W25–Tue

Jonah 1:1-3–W42–Sun

Micah 6:8–W26–Tue

Micah 7:18–W52–Mon

Nahum 1:3–W28–Thu

Habakkuk 2:2–W41–Tue

Habakkuk 2:20–W9–Sun

Zephaniah 3:17–W19–Mon

Haggai 1:2–W24–Tue

Haggai 2:9–W2–Mon

Zechariah 4:6–W44–Tue

Malachi 3:18–W35–Fri

Matthew 3:3–W48–Sun

Matthew 4:23–W5–Sun

Matthew 4:24–W37–Sun

Matthew 6:3-4–W21–Fri

Matthew 7:13-14–W48–Fri

Matthew 9:12-13–W43–Tue

Matthew 9:36–W23–Sun

Matthew 9:38–W2–Fri

Matthew 11:25–W19–Tue

Matthew 12:34–W36–Sun

Matthew 14:29–W10–Mon

Matthew 16:18–W12–Sun

Matthew 24:12–W2–Sun

Matthew 25:21–W42–Thu

Matthew 26:30–W13–Fri

Matthew 27:46–W12–Wed

Matthew 27:51–W13–Wed

Mark 4:15–W20–Fri

Mark 6:48–W48–Thu

Mark 8:29–W5–Mon

Mark 10:51–W38–Mon

Luke 2:7–W51–Fri

Luke 2:13–W51–Tue

Luke 2:14–W51–Wed

Luke 3:23–W28–Sun

Luke 8:3–W26–Thu

Luke 9:33–W52–Fri

Luke 10:20–W45–Wed

Luke 10:42–W39–Wed

Luke 11:1–W44–Sun

Luke 11:1–W50–Tue

Luke 11:8–W35–Sun

Luke 11:11-13–W35–Thu

Luke 12:15–W47–Fri

Luke 15:4–W42–Wed

Luke 15:17–W44–Thu

Luke 15:20–W25–Sun

Luke 21:28–W17–Tue

Luke 22:31-32–W25–Wed

John 1:17–W11–Wed

John 3:7–W26–Wed

John 3:8–W29–Mon

John 4:17-18–W31–Tue

John 6:12–W21–Mon

John 6:68-69–W10–Tue

John 8:32–W40–Sun

John 8:50–W49–Sun

John 10:10–W29–Sun

John 10:29b–W1–Tue

John 11:42–W13–Sun

John 11:44–W38–Wed

John 12:14–W13–Mon

John 13:14–W13–Thu

John 14:15-17–W49–Thu

John 14:23–W27–Wed

John 15:5–W21–Wed

John 15:11–W11–Mon

John 15:26–W45–Tue

John 17:4–W15–Thu

John 17:23–W5–Fri

John 19:39–W46–Mon

John 21:22–W4–Mon

Acts 1:9–W19–Thu

Acts 2:41–W23–Mon

Acts 3:19–W7–Fri

Acts 4:29-30–W9–Mon

Acts 5:41–W46–Fri

Acts 7:22–W25–Mon

Acts 10:34-35–W44–Fri

Acts 16:30–W23–Fri

Acts 17:11–W50–Thu

Acts 21:11–W34–Tue

Romans 2:1–W48–Mon

Romans 5:1–W47–Wed

Romans 5:5–W43–Mon

Romans 5:8–W7–Tue

Romans 6:23–W33–Thu

Romans 7:21–W48–Tue

Romans 8:1–W6–Fri

Romans 8:1–W35–Mon

Romans 8:16–W1–Thu

Romans 8:25–W11–Fri

Romans 8:31-32–W18–Sun

Romans 10:9–W35–Wed

Romans 12:21–W22–Sun

Romans 15:7–W37–Mon

Romans 16:1–W10–Fri

I Corinthians 1:23–W7–Sun

I Corinthians 1:27–W49–Fri

I Corinthians 6:19-20–
W10–Thu

I Corinthians 10:23–W10–Sun

I Corinthians 12:22-23–
W30–Tue

I Corinthians 13:11–W30–Wed

I Corinthians 15:13-14–
W14–Mon

I Corinthians 15:33–W20–Sun

I Corinthians 15:55–W50–Sun

2 Corinthians 1:3-4–W5–Thu

2 Corinthians 2:15–W40–Wed

2 Corinthians 3:4-6–W49–Wed

2 Corinthians 4:7–W11–Sun

2 Corinthians 4:16–W7–Mon

2 Corinthians 5:7–W52–Tue

2 Corinthians 13:11–W32–Mon

Galatians 2:20–W1–Fri

Galatians 5:7–W37–Wed

Galatians 6:1–W39–Thu

Galatians 6:2–W51–Sun

Galatians 6:9–W24–Sun

Ephesians 2:8–W4–Wed

Ephesians 3:17–W30–Sun

Ephesians 3:18–W36–Thu

Ephesians 4:3–W30–Fri

Ephesians 4:4–W33–Tue

Ephesians 5:18–W21–Sun

Philippians 1:18–W25–Fri

Philippians 1:29–W32–Tue

Philippians 2:5–W30–Thu

Philippians 2:28–W49–Mon

Philippians 3:10–W39–Mon

Philippians 3:13–W4–Sun

Philippians 3:20–W50–Fri

Philippians 4:8–W15–Sun

Philippians 4:13–W21–Thu

Philippians 4:19–W27–Tue

Colossians 2:6-7–W14–Thu

Colossians 4:5–W8–Fri

Colossians 4:12–W4–Tue

I Thessalonians 2:20–W19–Fri

I Thessalonians 4:1–W52–Wed

I Thessalonians 5:12–W20–Mon

I Thessalonians 5:17–W27–Fri

2 Thessalonians 1:8-9–
W41–Mon

2 Thessalonians 2:7-8–
    W21–Tue

I Timothy 4:12–W24–Wed

I Timothy 4:13–W4–Fri

I Timothy 6:17–W41–Fri

2 Timothy 1:7–W15–Fri

2 Timothy 2:3–W22–Mon

2 Timothy 3:5–W11–Tue

2 Timothy 3:12–W36–Tue

2 Timothy 4:2–W37–Fri

2 Timothy 4:11–W11–Thu

Titus 3:14–W12–Mon

Hebrews 2:15–W16–Tue

Hebrews 3:13–W9–Thu

Hebrews 4:7–W33–Wed

Hebrews 6:12–W47–Mon

Hebrews 7:25–W18–Mon

Hebrews 9:16-17–W18–Wed

Hebrews 11:1–W37–Thu

Hebrews 11:1-2–W16–Sun

Hebrews 12:2-3–W53–Sun

Hebrews 13:3–W8–Sun

Hebrews 13:5–W43–Sun

James 1:4–W34–Sun

James 1:27–W46–Sun

James 4:7–W23–Thu

James 5:16a–W9–Wed

James 5:16b–W31–Mon

I Peter 1:15–W12–Tue

I Peter 1:17–W8–Tue

I Peter 2:16–W27–Sun

I Peter 3:7–W37–Tue

I Peter 3:15–W28–Mon

I Peter 4:8–W24–Mon

2 Peter 3:18–W24–Fri

I John 3:1–W1–Wed

I John 4:18–W44–Wed

Jude 9–W31–Fri

Revelation 1:3–W2–Tue

Revelation 1:10–W3–Fri

Revelation 1:18–W14–Sun

Revelation 2:4–W28–Wed

Revelation 2:10–W3–Tue

Revelation 3:20–W46–Wed

Revelation 19:4–W41–Sun

Revelation 19:11–W42–Tue

Special Days–Index

TOPICS–INDEX

Salvation–W18Mon, W23Fri, W26Wed, W33Thu, W48Fri

Wait–W8Thu, W11Fri, W38Sun

Wonder–W33Fri, W40Fri

Word of God–W4Fri, W16Thu, W17Sun, W40Mon, W50Thu

Worship–W2Thu, W30Mon, W40Thu, W41Sun

CPSIA information can be obtained
at www.ICGtesting.com
Printed in the USA
LVHW021011091120
671147LV00004B/42

9 781632 211378